PIANO/VOCAL/CHORDS

100 years of Popular Music

1900 1920 1930 1940 1950 1960 1970 1980 1990 2000

CONTENTS

CONTENTS

Title | Page

AC-CENT-TCHU-ATE THE POSITIVE

Words by
JOHNNY MERCER

Music by
HAROLD ARLEN

F Dm Fm7 F7 Bb7
wan - na hear my sto - ry Then set - tle back and just sit tight
f
C7 Bbm Bb+ Cm Gm7 C7
While I start re - view - in' the at - ti - tude of do - in'
cantabile
Moderately (with a steady rock)
F Gm7 F Gm7
right.
very rhythmic
f
Refrain
Moderately (with a steady rock)
F F+ Dm F7 Bb Bbm Db11 G-9+ C9
You've got to AC-CENT-TCHU-ATE THE POS-I-TIVE, E - lim - my-nate the neg-a-tive,
mp - mf

F F+ Dm F7 Gm7 F Gm7 F
Latch on to the af-firm - a - tive, Don't mess with Mis - ter In - be - tween. _ You've got to
F F+ Dm F7 B♭ B♭m D♭11 G-9+ C9
spread joy up to the max - i - mum, Bring gloom down to the min - i - mum, _
F F+ Dm F7 Gm7 F Gm7 F
Have faith or pan - de-mo - ni - um li'- ble to walk up - on the scene. _ To il - lus -
very rhythmic
F C+ F9 F7+ B♭ C9 F Gm7 F
trate my last re - mark Jo - nah in the whale. No - ah in the Ark, _ What did they

F F9 D-9+ G9 C7+ F9 Db11 C9 C9+
do Just when ev-'ry-thing looked so dark? "Man," they said, "We bet-ter
F F+ Dm F7 Bb Bbm Db11 G-9+ C9
AC-CENT - TCHU-ATE THE POS-I-TIVE, E - lim - my-nate the neg-a-tive,
F F+ Dm F7 Gm7
Latch on to the af-firm-a-tive, Don't mess with Mis-ter In-be-
F D-9+ Gm7 C9 F Gm7 F F Gm7 F
tween." No! Don't mess with Mis-ter In-be-tween. You've got to tween.
1. 2.

ALL OR NOTHING AT ALL

Lyrics by
JACK LAWRENCE

Music by
ARTHUR ALTMAN

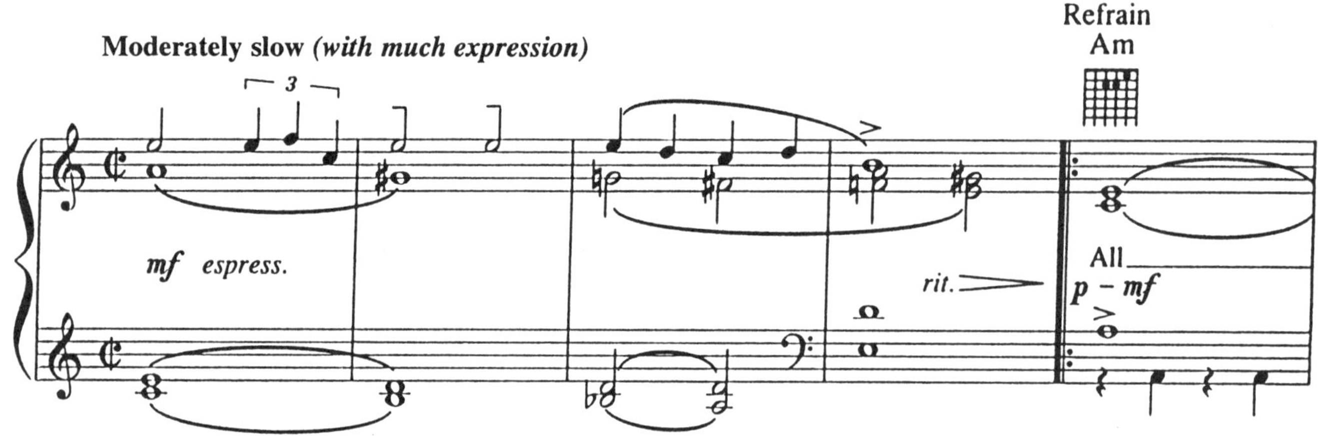

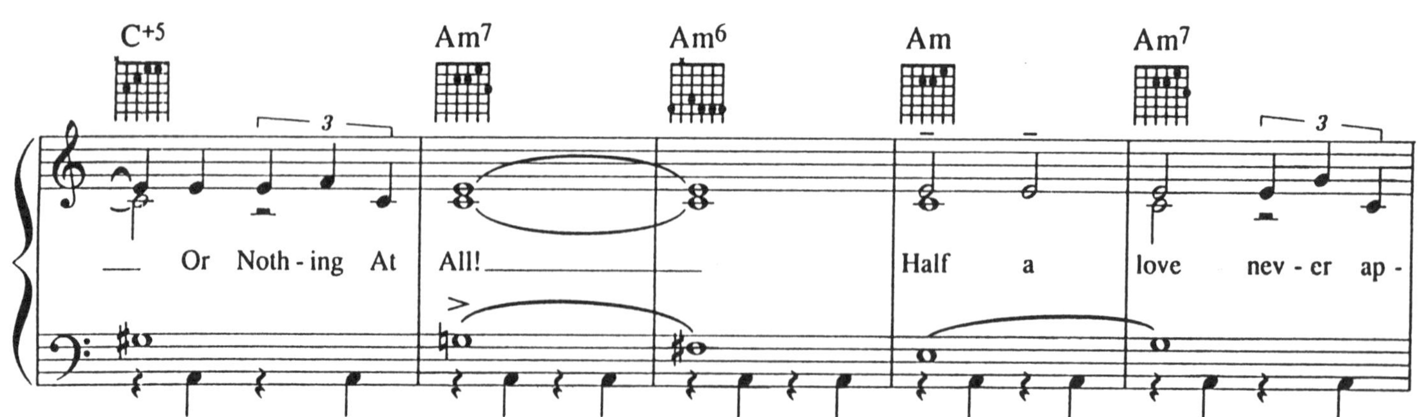

B♭7 B♭6 B♭+5 B♭7 Gm Gm6 Dm
fr5
pealed to me.
If your heart nev - er could yield to me,
G7 G7♭5 G7 Cmaj7 C6 Bm7 E7
then I'd rath - er have noth - ing at all!
Am C+5 Am7 Am6 Am
p
All Or Noth - ing At All!
If it's
Am7 B♭7 B♭6 B♭+5 B♭7 Gm Gm6
fr5
love there is no in be - tween.
Why be - gin, then cry for some - thing that

Dm
G7
G7♭5
G7
Cmaj7
C6
might have been.
No, I'd rath - er have noth - ing at all.
E♭9
E♭7
A♭
A♭+5
A♭6
A♭+5
A♭
A♭+5
A♭6
E♭7
But, please, don't bring your lips so close to my cheek.
Don't
mf espress.
A♭
A♭+5
D♭
A♭
E♭7
Cm6
E♭7
B♭m7
E♭7
smile or I'll be lost be-yond re - call.
The kiss in your eyes, the
B♭m7
E♭7
B♭m7
E♭7
B♭m6
C7
Fm
D♭7
touch of your hand makes me weak,
and my heart may grow diz - zy and

C7
E7
Am
C+5
Am7
fall. And if I fell un - der the spell of your call,
p
Am6
Am
Am7
B♭7
B♭6
B♭+5
B♭7
I would be caught in the un - der - tow.
Gm
Gm6
Dm
Dm6
E7
Am
So, you see, I've got to say: No! No! All
molto espress.
Fm6
1.
C
E7
2.
C
C6
Or Noth - ing At All! All!
f
f

From the Broadway Musical Production "BRIGADOON"

ALMOST LIKE BEING IN LOVE

Lyrics by
ALAN JAY LERNER

Music by
FREDERICK LOEWE

F7 F F+ Bb Cm7 Eb F7 Bb
face for the whole hu-man race. Why, it's al-most like be-ing in love!
Am7 D rit. Bdim. Am7 D+ G Eb
All the mu - sic of life seems to be, Like a bell that is
Am7-5b D7 Bb+ D7 Bdim. Eb F7 F F+
ring-ing for me. And from the way that I feel when that bell starts to
Bb Cm7 Eb7 Bb Gm Gb7 Bb Gm6b
peal I would swear I was fall-ing, I could swear I was fall-ing, It's al - most like
Gm D5b F7 Bb Fm7 Fm6 Fm7 Bb7 Bb
be-ing in love. What a love.
L.H.
rit.

AS TIME GOES BY

Words and Music by
HERMAN HUPFELD

Eb Eb7 Ab 4fr. C7 Fm
mf-f poco a poco cresc.
Moon - light and love _ songs nev - er out of date, Hearts full of pas - sion,
mf-f poco a poco cresc.
A°7 Cm 3fr. Ab7 4fr F7 Bb7 E°7
poco rit.
jeal - ous - y and hate; Wo - man needs man _ and man must have his mate, That no one can de -
poco rit.
Bb7 Fm7 Bb7 Bbm6 Bb7
p-mf a tempo
ny It's still the same old sto - ry, a fight for love and glo - ry, A
p-mf a tempo
Eb Bb+ Eb Gm 3fr. F7
case of do or die! The world will al - ways wel - come
1. 2.
Eb E°7 Fm7 Bb7 Bb7+5 Eb Cm 3fr F7 Bb7 Eb Db7 4fr. Eb
mf
lov - ers, As time goes by. You by. _
f mf f

AT LAST

Lyric by
MACK GORDON

Music by
HARRY WARREN

Fmaj7
G7-9
Cmaj7
C6
B
Am6
B7-9
Em
Am6
dream that I can speak to, A dream that I can call my own, I found a
Cm6
D7
Gmaj7
G6
C
Am7
D7-9
G
Dm7
G7
thrill to press my cheek to, A thrill I've nev - er known. You
C
Am
Dm7
G9
Dm7
C
Am
smiled and then the spell was cast
Dm7
G7+5
G7
C
Am
Dm7
G7-9
G7
And here we are in heav - en For you are mine At
1.
C
Am
Dm
G7-9
G7
Last. At
2.
C6
Fm6
G7-9
C6
Last. rit.
Ped.
*

ALL OF A SUDDEN MY HEART SINGS

English Words by HAROLD ROME
French Lyric by JAMBLAN

Music by
LAURENT HERPIN

Slow rock

Am Em Dm7 G7

f

C G7

mp

All of a sud-den my heart sings, when I re-mem-ber lit-tle things;
All of a sud-den my heart sings, when I re-mem-ber lit-tle things;

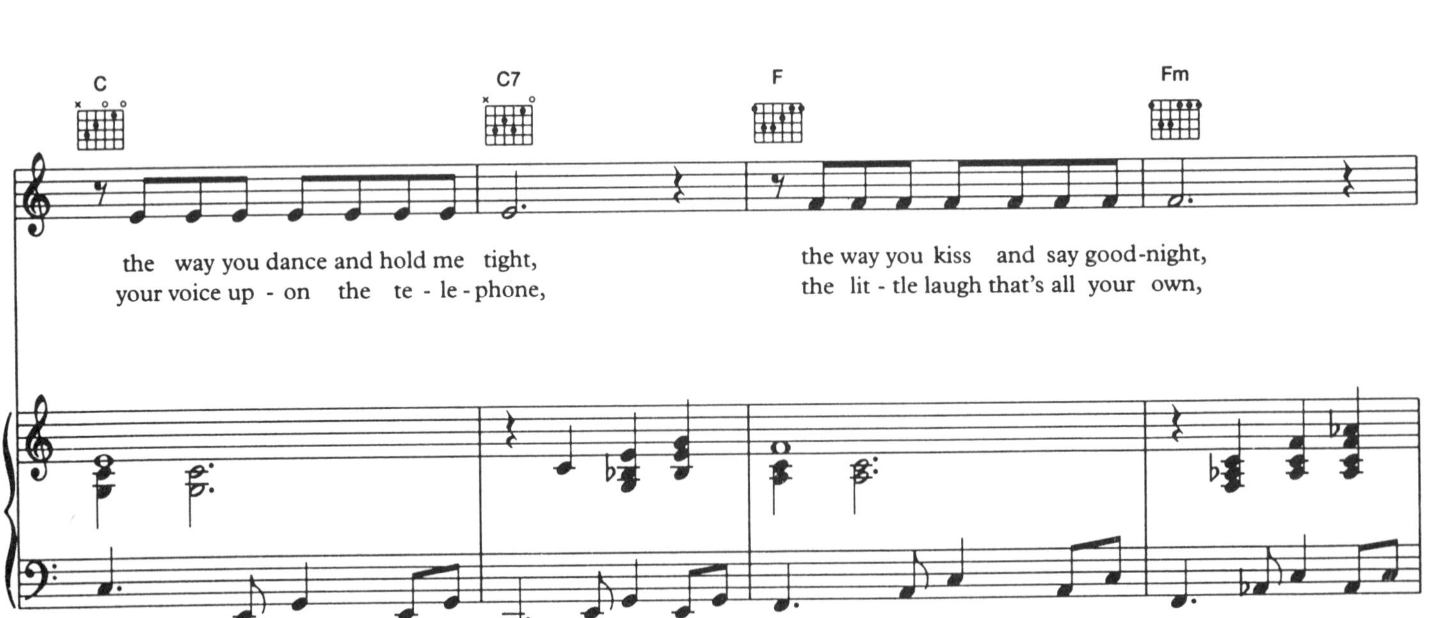

C
C7
F
the cra-zy things we say and do,
the fun it is to be with you,
the way a smile lights up your eyes,
the way you look up in sur-prise,
G7
C
the ma-gic thrill that's in your touch,
oh dar-ling, I love you so much,
the ma-gic thrill that's in your touch,
oh dar-ling, I love you so much,
Am
Em
the sec-ret way you press my hand,
to let me know you un-der-stand,
the fun-ny way you hold your head,
the cra-zy things you've of-ten said,
F
G7
C
A7
the wind and rain up - on your face,
the breath-less world of your em-brace,
the way your hair won't stay in place,
the wind and rain up-on your face,

Dm7
Fm
C6
A7
your lit - tle laugh and half sur - prise,
the way you hold my hand at shows,
the star-light gleam-ing in your eyes,
the way you wrin - kle up your nose,
D7
1.
G7
C
Dm7
C6
re-mem-bering all those lit - tle things,
re-mem-bering all those lit - tle
all of a sud-den my heart sings.
2.
G7
C
rit.
G11
G7
C
F6/C
C
things,
all of a sud-den my heart sings.

BABY, WON'T YOU PLEASE COME HOME

Words and Music by
CHARLES WARFIELD and CLARENCE WILLIAMS

Dm7
G9
C
Em7
A7
Dmaj7
E♭dim
Ask you won't you please come home 'Cause when you're gone I'm all for- lorn, I
Em7
A7-5
D7
Am7
A♭7
C
F♯m7
wor - ry all day long:
Ba - by, won't you please come
mp-mf
F9
E9
A7
Em7
A7
home, 'Cause your mam - ma's all a - lone
D7
Em
A7
E♭9
I have tried in vain, nev - er no more to call, your name

D9 G F#m7 B7 E7
When you left you broke my heart Be -
Am7 C C7 B7 C C#dim
cause I nev - er thought we'd part. Ev - 'ry hour in the day, you will
G F7 E7 A7 D7 1 G A7 Ab9
hear me say, Ba - by won't you please come home
2 G B7 E7 Am7 D7 Ab7 G
home Dad - dy needs mam - ma, Ba - by won't you please come home.

BABY FACE

Words and Music by
BENNY DAVIS and
HARRY AKST

G7
D7
B♭o7
G9
3fr.
G7
Cmaj7
You sure have start - ed some - thin'. Ba - by Face,
3
C6
A
E7
D7
E7
Am
I'm up in heav - en when I'm in your fond em - brace.
Gm7
C7
F6
F♯o7
C
E7
A7
I did - n't need a shove 'cause I just fell in love
C
Dm7
Dmaj7+5
G13
C6
with your pret - ty ba - by face.

BEAT ME DADDY, EIGHT TO THE BAR

Words and Music by
DON RAYE, HUGHIE PRINCE and ELEANOR SHEEHY

B♭
B♭7
Bdim7
but the style he likes the best is eight to the bar.
F7
When he plays it's a ball, he's the dad - dy of them
B♭
E♭6
B♭
B♭
all.
The peo - ple gath - er a - round when he
B♭7
gets on the stand, then when he plays he gets a hand. The

E♭
3fr
B♭
rhy - thm he beats puts the cats in a trance, no - bod - y there
F7
both - ers to dance. But when he jams with the bass and gui - tar,
B♭
C♯dim7
Cm7
3fr
F7
B♭
they hol - ler, "Aw, beat me, dad - dy, eight to the bar." A
plink, a plank, a plink plank plink plank plunk - in' on the keys,

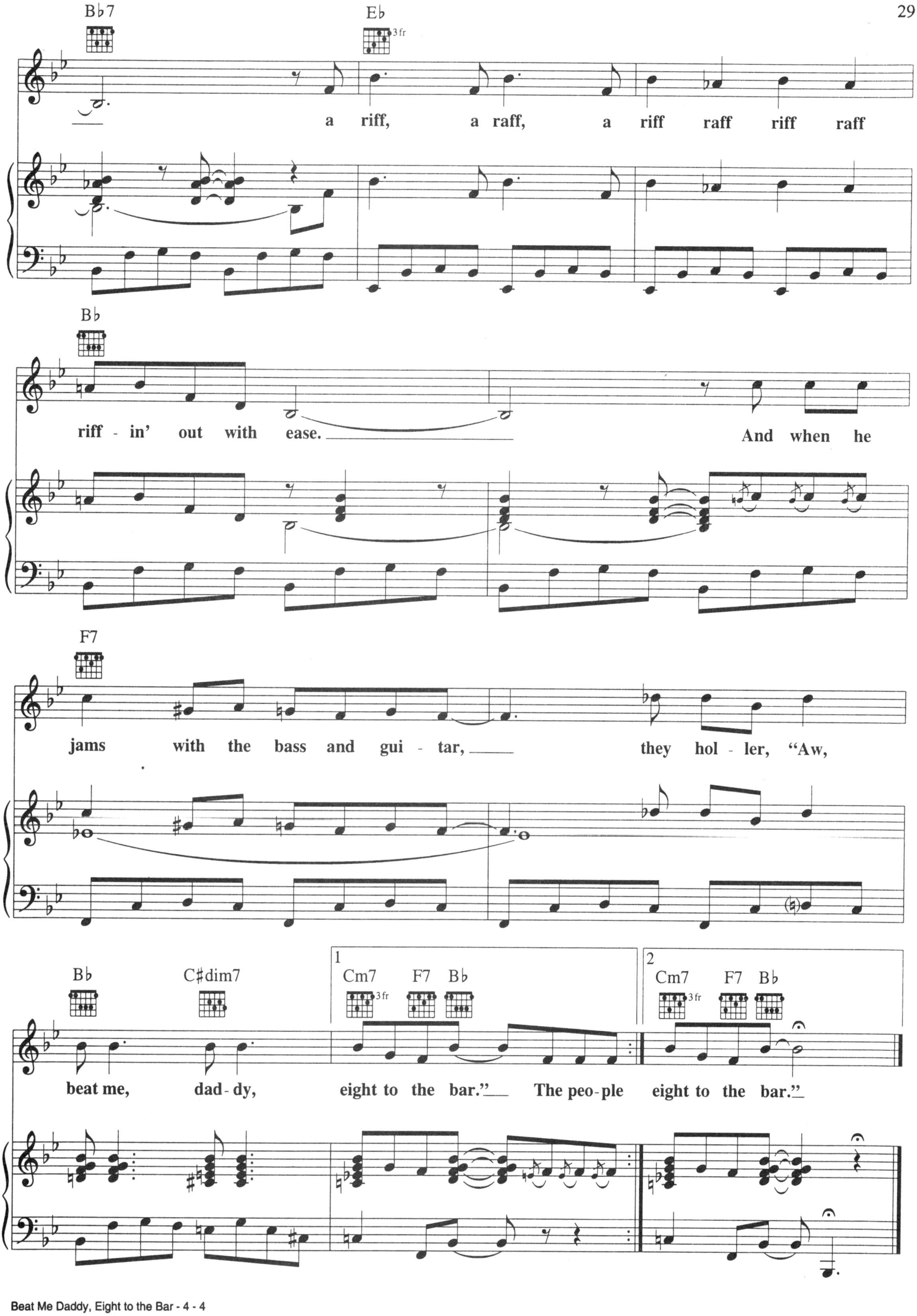
B♭7
E♭
3 fr
a riff, a raff, a riff raff riff raff
B♭
riff - in' out with ease.
And when he
F7
jams with the bass and gui - tar,
they hol - ler, "Aw,
B♭
C♯dim7
1
Cm7
3 fr
F7
B♭
2
Cm7
3 fr
F7
B♭
beat me, dad - dy, eight to the bar." The peo - ple eight to the bar."

BEWITCHED

Words by
LORENZ HART

Music by
RICHARD RODGERS

Dm7
G7
C
Dm7
G7
C
A7
Love's the same old sad sen - sa - tion, Late - ly I've not slept a wink,
Dm7
G7
C
Dm7
G7
Since this half-pint im - i - ta - tion, Put me on the blink.
rall.
Refrain (slowly)
C
G7
C
C+
I'm wild a - gain, Be - guiled a - gain, A sim - per - ing, whim - per - ing
p
F
G♯dim
C
D7
G7
A7
child a - gain, Be - witched, both - ered and be - wild - ered am

Dm
G7
C
G7
I.
Could - n't sleep, And would - n't sleep, When
C
C+
F
G♯dim
C
D7
love came and told me I should - n't sleep, Be - witched, both - ered and be -
G7
C7
F
A7
wild - ered am I.
A7
Am
Lost my heart, but what of it? He is cold I a -
mp

G7 sus.4
G7
C
F#dim
gree, He can laugh, but I love it, Al-though the laugh's on
mf
Dm7
G7
C
G7
C
C+
me. I'll sing to him, Each spring to him, And long for the day when I'll
p
F
G#dim
C
D7
Dm
G7
cling to him, Be - witched, both - ered and be - wild - ered am
1. C
Am
Dm7
G7
2. C
F
C
I. I'm I.
sf

BLUES IN THE NIGHT

(My Mama Done Tol' Me)

Lyrics by
JOHNNY MERCER

Music by
HAROLD ARLEN

Bb
Bb7
F7+5
Bbm7
Eb7
blues in the night, Now the rain's a-fall-in', hear the train a-call-in', whoo-ee, (My
Eb9
Ebm6
F7
ma-ma done tol' me,) Hear dat lone-some whis-tle blow-in' 'cross the tres-tle, whoo-ee, (My
C7
ma-ma done tol' me,) A whoo-ee-duh-whoo-ee, Ol' click-e-ty clack's a-ech-o-in' back th'
blues in the night, The eve-nin' breeze-'ll start the trees to cry-in' and the
broadly

Db7
C+
C7
G+
G7 b5
Bbm6
C7
F7
Ebm6
moon - 'll hide its light, when you get the blues in the night.
R. H.
Abm6
F 7
Eb9
Ebm6
F7
Db7
Take my word, the mock - in' bird -'ll sing the sad - dest kind o'
C+
C7
G+
G-5
Bbm6
C7
F7
Ebm6
song, he knows things are wrong and he's right.
R. H.
Abm6
F7
Bb7
C7
F7
Bb
(whistle)
From Nat-chez to Mo-bile, from

Bb7
Eb7
Mem-phis to St. Joe, — where - ev - er the four winds blow; — I been in some big towns — an'
C7
F7
F+
Bb
F7
heard me some big talk, — but there is one thing I know, —
A wom-an's a two-face, —
A man is a two-face, —
A
C7
F7
Bb
wor - ri - some thing who'll leave ya t' sing the blues — in the night. Hum —
Bb7
C7 b9
F7
C7
F7 sus.4
Bb
My ma - ma was right, there's blues — in the night.
ppp

BODY AND SOUL

Words by
EDWARD HEYMAN, ROBERT SOUR
and FRANK EYTON
French Words by EMELIA RENAUD
Spanish Words by JOHNNIE CAMACHO

Music by
JOHNNY GREEN

F♯m B7 A F♯m7
To leave me here all a - lone
Pour m'a-ban-don-ner ain - si.
No im-por-ta lo mis-mo dá
When you could make my life worth
Je pour-rais a - voir tant de
Es - cu - cha so - lo un mo -
Bm E7 E7 sus A A7 +5
un poco rall.
liv - ing By sim - ply tak - ing what I'm set on giv - ing.
bon - heur Si tu vou-lais sim-ple-ment pren-dre mon coeur.
men - to, Y te di - ré las an - sias que yo sien - to:
un poco rall.
REFRAIN (Slowly, with expression)
Dm p-mf G7 susC G7 C G7+ C Cdim
My heart is sad and lone-ly, For you I sigh, for you, dear, on - ly.
Mon coeur est dé - ses - pé - ré. Pour toi il ne fait que sou - pi - rer
No nie-gues el re - cuer-do de nues-tro a-mor que fué sin - ce - ro.
p-mf
Dm G7 E7 Am Dm G7
Why have-n't you seen it? I'm all for you, Bod - y and
Ne sais tu pas dé - jà Que je t'ai - me pas-sion-né -
¿No vés que te quie - ro, Que es pa - ra tí, to - do mi

C Am C Am Dm G7 susC G7 C G7+
Soul! I spend my days in long-ing And won-d'ring why it's
ment? Je me de-man-de tou-jours Pour quoi il n'y a
ser? Los be-sos que me dis-te No de-jan que hoy mi
mf-f
p-mf
C Cdim Dm7 G7 E7 Am Dm7 G7
me you're wrong-ing, I tell you I mean it, I'm all for you, Bod-y and
plus de beaux jours, Crois moi quand je te dis Que je t'ai-me pas-sion-né-
al-ma ol-vi-de lo que me qui-sis-te. Que es pa-ra tí. to-do mi
C Am Ab7 Db mp-mf Ab7 Db Gb
Soul! I can't be-lieve it, It's hard to con-ceive it That
ment! Je ne puis croi-re, Ni mê-me con-ce-voir Que
ser. Yo quie-ro a-mar-te, vol-ver a be-sar-te, y ha-
mf-f
mp-mf
Db Ab7 Db C♯m7 F♯7
you'd turn a-way ro-mance. Are you pre-tend-ing, it
tu é-lu-des l'a-mour. Veux tu pré-ten-dre que
blar-te de mi pa-sión. Si tú me quie-res, en-
mf-f

Bma7 B C♯m7 F♯7 B7 B♭7 un poco rall. A7
looks like the end-ing Un-less I could have one more chance to prove, dear,
c'est le dé-noue-ment, Faut-il à ja-mais nous sé-pa-rer, che-ri?
ton-ces no de-jes que llo-re, por tu co-ra-zón, mi vi-da,
un poco rall.
Dm p-mf G7 sus C G7 C G7+
My life a wreck you're mak-ing, You know I'm yours for
Mon cœur est con-ci-li-ant, Et d'a-mour pour toi
De hi-no-jos yo te pi-do, Que si u-na vez yo
p-mf
C Cdim Dm7 G7 E7 Am Dm7 G7
just the tak-ing; I'd glad-ly sur-ren-der my-self to you, Bod-y and
il est rem-pli; Je ne veux que t'ai-mer pas-sion-né-ment, pas-sion-né-
te he men-ti-do, que tu me per-do-nes; Y te da-ré to-do mi
1. C A7
Soul!
ment!
ser.
2. C D♭ C D♭ C
Soul!
ment!
ser.
mf
mf
f

BOY MEETS HORN

Words and Music by
DUKE ELLINGTON, IRVING MILLS
and REX STEWART

C dim E7 C C dim
mel - o - dy so new when BOY MEETS HORN; low and oh, so
G E7 C A7 G Eb7 D7
sweet that it seems It's like the mel - low mus - ic from an - oth - er world of dreams; you'll hear a
G Em G7 E7 C dim E7
strange and ten - der tune when - ev - er BOY MEETS HORN, and when the mus - ic in the moon - light
Am Eb
greets the morn, you'll see him stand - ing way a bove the crowd and rock - in on a
D7 F dim D7 1. D7 G 2. D7 G
cloud when - ev - er BOY MEETS HORN, you'll hear a BOY MEETS HORN.

BOOGIE WOOGIE BUGLE BOY

Words and Music by
DON RAYE and HUGHIE PRINCE

G7
F7
ar - my now a - blow - in' re - veil - le, He's the
C
BOO - GIE WOO - GIE BU - GLE BOY of Com - pa - ny B. They
C
1. made him blow a bu - gle for his Un - cle Sam, It real - ly brought him down be - cause he
2. puts the boys to sleep with "boo - gie" ev - 'ry night, And wakes them up the same way in the
C7
F
could - n't jam. The cap - tain seemed to un - der - stand Be - cause the
ear - ly bright. They clap their hands and stamp their feet Be - cause they
C
G7
next day the "cap" went out and draft - ed a band, And now the comp - 'ny jumps when he plays re - veil - le, He's the
know how he plays when some - one gives him a beat, He real - ly breaks it up

C
BOO-GIE WOO-GIE BU-GLE BOY of Com-pa-ny B__ A toot! A toot! A
toot did-dle ah-da toot. He blows it eight to the bar__ in "boo-gie" rhy-thm. He
F
C
can't blow a note un-less a bass and gui-tar__ is play-in' with 'im.
G7
F7
He makes the comp-'ny jump when he plays re-veil-le, He's the
C
1.
2.
BOO-GIE WOO-GIE BU-GLE BOY of Com-pa-ny B.__ He Com-pa-ny B.__

DEARLY BELOVED

Words by
JOHNNY MERCER

Music by
JEROME KERN

Refrain-Andante cantabile, ma ben ritmato
G
F
G
F
Dear - ly be - lov - ed, how clear - ly I see,
mp
G
F
Dm7
G
G9
Some - where in Heav - en you were fash - ioned for me,
cresc.
C
Dm7
G7
Dm7
G7
An - gel eyes knew you,
mf
Cmaj.7
ten.
Gdim
C6
Em
Ab9
Ab7
An - gel voi - ces led me to you;
ten.

G
F
G
F
Noth - ing could save me, Fate gave me a sign;
G
F
Dm7
G
G9
I know that I'll be yours come show - er or shine;
C
D7
G7
Gdim
So I say merely, Dearly be -
rall. e dim.
Dm7
G7
1.
C
B♭7
2.
C
lov - ed be mine.
mine.
a tempo
L.H.

CHATTANOOGA CHOO-CHOO

Lyric by
MACK GORDON

Music by
HARRY WARREN

Dm7
G7
G9
C
I've got my fare — and just a tri-fle to spare.
C7
Bb(C sus)
C7
F
C7
F
Gm7
C7
F
C7
You leave the Penn-syl-va-nia sta-tion 'bout a quar-ter to four, — read — a mag-a-zine and then you're
mf
F
F9
Bb
Fdim
F
D+
D7
G-9
in Bal-ti-more, — Din-ner in the din-er, noth-ing could be fin-er than — to have your ham'n eggs in
Abm6
C9
F
C7
F
Gm7
C7
Car-o-li-na. When — you hear the whis-tle blow-in' eight to the bar — Then —

F
C7
F
F9
B♭
Fdim
F
D+
D7
— you know that Ten-nes-see is not ver-y far, — Shov - el all the coal in, got - ta keep it roll-in'
G-9
C7
F
G7
C
Woo, Woo, Chat - ta-noo - ga there — you are. —
mp
C
Cdim
C6
There's gon-na be — a cer-tain par-ty at the sta-tion — Sat - in and lace, —
Dm7
G7
G9
C
— I used to call fun - ny face. —

Cdim
C6
C7
F
She's gon - na cry until I tell her that I'll nev - er roam,
Ab7
D7-5
C
Am7
D7
Dm7
G-9
C
So Chat - ta-noo - ga Choo-Choo won't you choo-choo me home.
Cm6
C7
(A sus)
Cm6
C7
Am7
Chat - ta-noo - ga Choo-Choo won't
D7-5
Dm7
G-9
C
G7
C
C
(Single note)
you choo - choo me home.
sfz

DON'T SIT UNDER THE APPLE TREE

(With Anyone Else but Me)

Words and Music by
CHARLIE TOBIAS, LEW BROWN
and SAM H. STEPT

Chorus, Brightly
F
C7
F
D7-9
Don't Sit Un-der The Ap-ple Tree with an-y-one else but me,
mp
Gm7
C7
Gm7
C7
F
Gm7
C7
F
C7
Gm7
C7
An-y-one else but me, An-y-one else but me, No! No! No!
F
C7
F
Cm6
D7
Just re-mem-ber that I've been true to no-bod-y else but you, So
G7
Gm7
C7
F
Bb
F
Gm7
just be true to me.

F
C7
F
D7-9
Don't go walk-ing down lov-ers' lane with an-y-one else but me,
Gm7
C7
Gm7
C7
F
Gm7
C7
F
C7
Gm7
C7
An-y-one else but me,
An-y-one else but me, No! No! No!
F
C7
F
Cm6
D7
Don't start show-ing off all your charms in some-bod-y else's arms, You
G7
Gm7
C7
F
Gm7
F
F7
Bb
must be true to me.
I'm so a-fraid that the
mf

Gm7
C9
F
C7
F
A7
Dm
Dm7
plans we made un-der - neath those moon-lit skies Will fade a - way and you're
Dm6
G9
C7
Dm7
Cdim
C7
C7+5
F
C7
bound to stray if the stars get in your eyes, So, Don't Sit Un-der The
F
F
Cm6
D7
G7
Ap-ple Tree with an-y - one else but me, You're my L -
Gm7
C7
1.
F
Bb
F
Cdim
Gm7
C7
2.
F
Bb6
F
O - V - E. E.

DREAM

Words and Music by
JOHNNY MERCER

Bb
F+
Bbmaj7
C7
Co
C9
Cm7
3fr.
F7
Cm7
3fr.
rise in the air, You'll find your share of mem - o - ries there.
Cm7
3fr.
F7-5
Bb
A7
So DREAM when the day is thru,
Bb
Dm7
G7
Eb
DREAM and they might come true, Things
Ebm
Bb
A7
D7
Gm7
3fr.
Cm7
3fr.
F7-9
never are as bad as they seem, So DREAM, DREAM,
1.Bb
F13
F7sus4
F7-9
2.Bb
F7-9
Bb6add9
DREAM. DREAM.
rall.

DON'T GET AROUND MUCH ANYMORE

Lyric by
BOB RUSSELL

Music by
DUKE ELLINGTON

Chorus, Slowly
Guitar Tacit
C
A9
Missed the Sat - ur - day dance Heard they crowd-ed the floor
mf
Am7
D7
G7
C
Could - n't bear it with - out you Don't Get A - round Much An - y - more
Guitar Tacit
C
A9
Thought I'd vis - it the club Got as far as the door
Am7
D7
G7
C
They'd have asked me a - bout you Don't Get A - round Much An - y - more

F
Fm
Em7
C
C7
C7+5
Dar - ling I guess my mind's more at ease But
mf
F
Am6
B7
Em
B
G7
Guitar Tacit
C
nev - er-the - less Why stir up mem-o - ries Been in-vit - ed on dates
A9
Am7
D7
Might have gone but what for Aw - f'lly dif-f'rent with - out you
G7
1. C
2. C
Guitar Tacit
Don't Get A - round Much An - y - more. Missed the Sat - ur - day more.
mf
p

EVERYBODY LOVES SOMEBODY

Lyric by
IRVING TAYLOR

Music by
KEN LANE

Chorus
Slowly
F
F+
B♭
D7
Gm
E♭
C7
Ev-'ry-bod-y loves some bod-y some-time,
Ev-'ry-bod-y falls in love some- how.
mp
Abdim
Gm7
C+
Some- thing in your kiss just told me my some- time is now.
Ev-'ry-bod- y finds some-bod-y some place,
There's no tell-ing where love may ap- pear.
C7-9
Some-thing in my heart keeps say- ing my some - place is here.

F7
Cm7
F7
B♭
F+
B♭
B♭dim
B♭
If I had it in my pow-er I'd ar- range for ev-'ry girl to have your charms.
Dm
A+
Dm7
G7
Gm7
Cdim
Gm7
C7
Then ev-'ry min- ute, ev-'ry hour Ev-'ry boy would find what I found in your arms.
F
F+
B♭
D7
Gm
E♭
C7
Ev-'ry-bod-y loves some-bod-y some-time, And al-though my dream was o- ver - due,
F
A♭dim
Gm7
C7
C7-9
F
Gm7
C7
F
Your love made it well worth wait-ing for some-one like you. you.
rit.
p

FOOLS RUSH IN
(Where Angels Fear To Tread)

Lyrics by
JOHNNY MERCER

Music by
RUBE BLOOM

Dm7
G7
C
Am7
Chorus, Slowly (with expression)
Fools rush in where an-gels fear to tread, and so I come to
mp mf
you, my love, my heart a - bove my head. Though I
F
D7-5
D7
G
Dm7 (G Bass)
see the dan - ger there, if there's a
chance for me then I don't care. Fools rush in
f

G7
C
Am7
Dm7
where wise men nev-er go, but wise men nev - er fall in love
Bb7-5
A7
Dm
so how are they to know? When we met
Fm6
Am
I felt my life be-gin; so o - pen up your heart, and let
Fm6
Ab
Ab7
this fool rush in. in.

(I Love You)

FOR SENTIMENTAL REASONS

Words by
DEEK WATSON

Music by
WILLIAM BEST

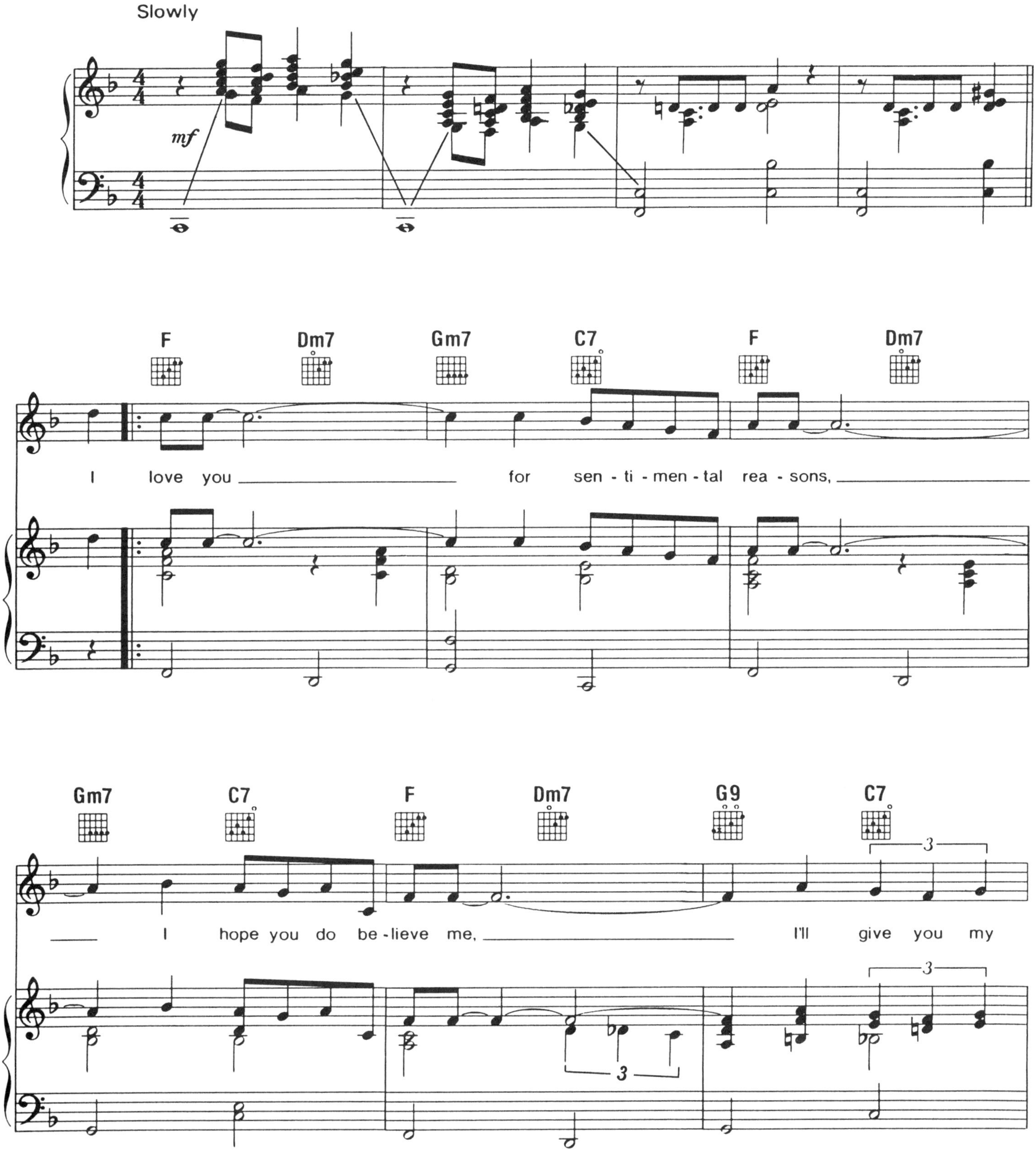

Slowly

mf

F Dm7 Gm7 C7 F Dm7

I love you ___ for sen - ti - men - tal rea - sons, ___

Gm7 C7 F Dm7 G9 C7

___ I hope you do be - lieve me, ___ I'll give you my

F D7 Gm7 C7 C9+5 F Dm7 Gm7 C7
heart. I love you, and you a - lone were
F Dm7 Gm7 C7 F Dm7 Gm7 C7
meant for me, Please give your lov - ing heart to me, and say we'll nev - er
F Gm7 Fdim F Gm7 C7 F Cdim
part. I think of you ev - 'ry morn - ing,
Gm7 C7 F Dm Gm6 A7
dream of you ev - 'ry night; Darl - ing, I'm nev - er

Dm
Dm7
G9
C7
C9+5
lone - ly when - ev - er you're in sight. I
F
Dm7
Gm7
C7
F
Dm7
love you for sen - ti - men - tal rea - sons
Gm7
C7
F
Dm
G9
C7
I hope you do be - lieve me, I've giv - en you my
1
F
Gm7
Fdim
C7
C9+5
heart. I
2
F
Bbm
Db9
Fmaj7
heart.

FOR YOU, FOR ME, FOR EVERMORE

Music and Lyrics by
GEORGE GERSHWIN and IRA GERSHWIN

Cm
F9
Ab
Bb7
Eb
Ebdim
Fm7
Bb7
If we walk on air. All the shad-ows now will lose us,
Db
Eb7
Ab
G7
Cm
G+
Cm7
Luck - y stars are ev - 'ry - where. As a hap - py
F9
Fm7
poco rit.
Bb9
be - ing, Here's what I'm fore - see - ing:
poco rit.
Refrain (not fast)
Bb7
Eb
F7
Fm7
Bb7
Fm7
Bb7
For you, for me, for ev - er - more, It's
p - mf

Eb
F7
Fm7
Bb7
Fm7
Bb7
bound to be for ev - er - more. It's
Bbm7
Eb7
Bbm7
Eb7
plain to see, we found by find - ing each
Ab
Cm7
F7
B♮7
oth - er, The love we wait - ed for.
Bb+
Bb7
Eb
F7
Fm7
Bb7
I'm yours, you're mine, and in our hearts
mp

Fm7
B♭7
B♭m7
E♭7
A♭
The hap - py end - ing starts.
A♭m
E♭
Gm
Fm7
B♭7
What a love - ly world this world will be, With a
E♭
B♭
Cm7
F9
F7
Fm7
E♭
Fm7
B♭7
world of love in store For you, for me, for ev - er -
mf
1. E♭
Cm6
B♭7
2. E♭
more! For more!
mf
mf

GALWAY BAY

Words and Music by
DR. ARTHUR COLAHAN
Moderato
Refrain
F Gm7 C7
1. If you ev - er go a - cross the sea to Ire - land, Then
2.(For the) breez - es blow - ing o'er the seas from Ire - land, Are
F F7 D7
ten.
may-be at the clos - ing of your day, You will sit and watch the moon rise o - ver
per-fum'd by the heath - er as they blow, And the wo-men in the up - lands dig-gin'
G7 C7 F
Clad-dagh, — And see the sun go down on GAL-WAY BAY. Just to
pra - ties, Speak a lan - guage that the stran - gers do not know. For the
Gm7 C7
hear a-gain the rip - ple of the trout stream, The wo - men in the mea-dows mak-ing
stran-gers came and tried to teach us their way, They scorn'd us just for be - ing what we

F F7 D7 G7
ten.
hay, And to sit be-side a turf-fire in the cab-in, And
are, But they might as well go chas-ing aft-er moon-beams, Or
C7
1. F
2. F
watch the bare-foot gos-soons at their play. 2. For the
light a pen-ny can-dle from a star And if
Gm7 C7
there is going to be a life here-aft-er, And
F D7
Some-how I am sure there's going to be, I will ask my God to let me make my
G7 C7 F Bb6 F
heav-en, In that dear land a-cross the I-rish sea.
rit.

GIVE ME THE SIMPLE LIFE

Words by
HARRY RUBY

Music by
RUBE BLOOM

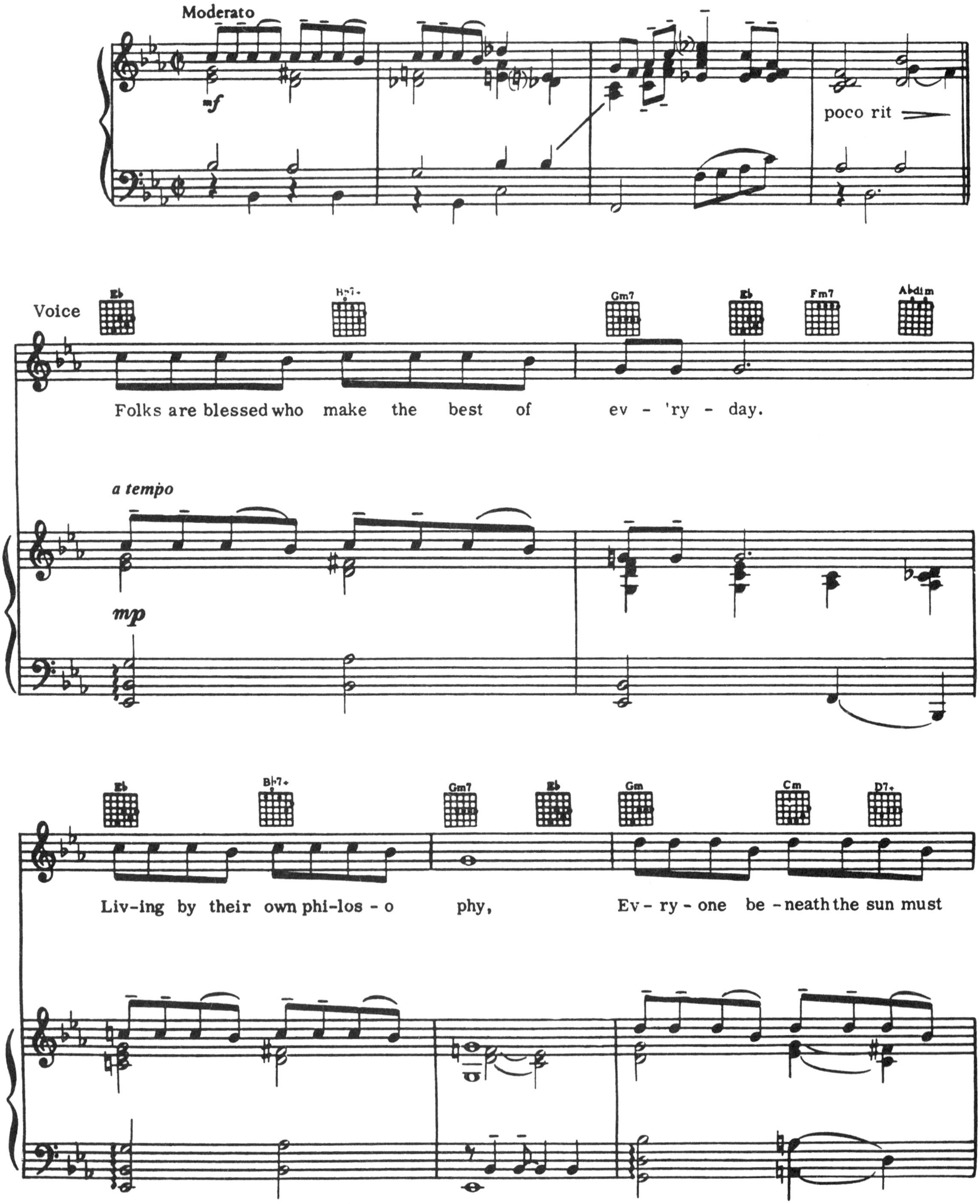

Moderato

mf

poco rit

Voice

Eb Bb7+ Gm7 Eb Fm7 Abdim

Folks are blessed who make the best of ev - 'ry - day.

a tempo

mp

Eb Bb7+ Gm7 Eb Gm Cm D7+

Liv-ing by their own phi-los - o phy, Ev - ry - one be - neath the sun must

Gm Fm Ab+ Fm7 Fm7 Abm Bb7
find a - way, — and I have found the on - ly way for me.
rit.
Fm7 Bb7 Ebmaj7 C7 Fm
Refrain Rhythmically, but not fast
I don't be - lieve in fret - tin' and griev - in'; why —
Liv - ing I find is best — when your mind is keen —
mp-f a tempo
G7 Cm G7 Eb7 Cm Abm Eb
— mess a - round with strife; — I nev - er was cut out to —
— as a carv - ing knife. — I'm cra - zy a - bout sleep, can't —
Cm Fm7 C9 F7 F7+ Bb9 Fm7
— step and strut out. Give — me the sim - ple life! — Some —
— do with - out sleep. Give — me the sim - ple life! — I —

Bb7 Ebmaj7 C7 Fm G7 Cm
find it pleas-ant din - ing on pheas-ant. Those things roll off my knife;
love to whit-tle and play a lit - tle tune on a ten-cent fife;
G7 Eb7 Cm Abm Eb Cm Fm7
just serve me to - ma - toes and mashed po - ta - toes; give
I don't aim to wor-ry, hus - tle or hur-ry; give
Bb7 Eb Fm7 Bb9
me the sim-ple life. A cot - tage small is all I'm
me the sim-ple life. I greet the dawn when I a -
Eb Fm7 Bb9 Eb
af - ter, not one that's spa - cious and wide. A
wak - en, the sky is clear up a - bove. I

Fm
G7-9
Cm
Cm7
F9
house that rings with joy and laugh-ter and the ones you love in -
like my scram-bled eggs and ba - con served by some - one that I
Fm7
Bb7
Fm7
Bb7
Ebmaj7
C7
Fm
side. Some like the high road, I like the low road, free
love. Life could be thrill - ing with one who's will - ing to
G7
Cm
G7
Eb7
Cm
Abm
Eb
from the care and strife. Sounds corn - y and seed - y, but
be a farm-er's wife; kids call - ing me pap - py would
Cm
Fm7
Bb7
Eb
1.
Ebdim
2.
yes, in-deed-y; give me the sim-ple life!
make me hap-py; give me the sim-ple life!
fz

HAVE I TOLD YOU LATELY THAT I LOVE YOU

Words and Music by
SCOTT WISEMAN

C
Fm
F
C
C+
F
C
now.
now.
now.
This heart would break in two if you re - fuse me,
Edim
G7
C
C+
I'm no good with - out you an - y - how.
Dear, have I
F
C
Edim
G7
told you late - ly that I love you,
Well, dar - ling, I'm
1.
C
Fm
G
C
Fm
3
C
Fm
C
tell - ing you now.
Have I
Have I
now.

HEARTACHES

Words by
JOHN KLENNER

Music by
AL HOFFMAN

G
B7
Em
I nev - er dreamt your words would prove un - true,
A7
Eb9+5
Am7
D9
Am7
D7+5
I was a fool to fall.
You brought me
G6
G
F#7
Heart - aches, heart - aches,
G
Dm6
My lov - ing you meant on - ly heart -

E7
Am7
D7
aches
Your kiss was such a sa - cred
G
Em
A7
thing to me,
I can't be -
Cm6
D7
D7
G6
lieve it's just a burn - ing mem - o - ry.
Heart -
G
F♯7
G
aches,
heart - aches,
What does it

G9
Gb9
F9
E9
mat - ter how my heart breaks?
Am7
Cm
Gdim
G
Bm
A7
I should be hap - py with some - one new,
Am7
D7
Am7
D7
D7-9
But my heart aches for
1
G
Am7
D7
you.
2
G
you.

HOW ABOUT YOU?

Words by
RALPH FREED

Music by
BURTON LANE

G
Gmaj7
G
B♭dim
Am7
D7
I'm mad a - bout good books, can't get my fill,
G9
Dm7
G9
Dm7
Cmaj7
C6
And Frank - lin Roose - velt's looks, give me a thrill.
Cm
G
E♭7
Hold - ing hands in a mov - ie show, when all the lights are low
Am
B7+5
B7
Em
Em7
C
D7
may not be new, But I like it, How A - bout
1.
G
Am7
D9
You?
2.
G
Am7
G
You?

HOW HIGH THE MOON

Words by
NANCY HAMILTON

Music by
MORGAN LEWIS

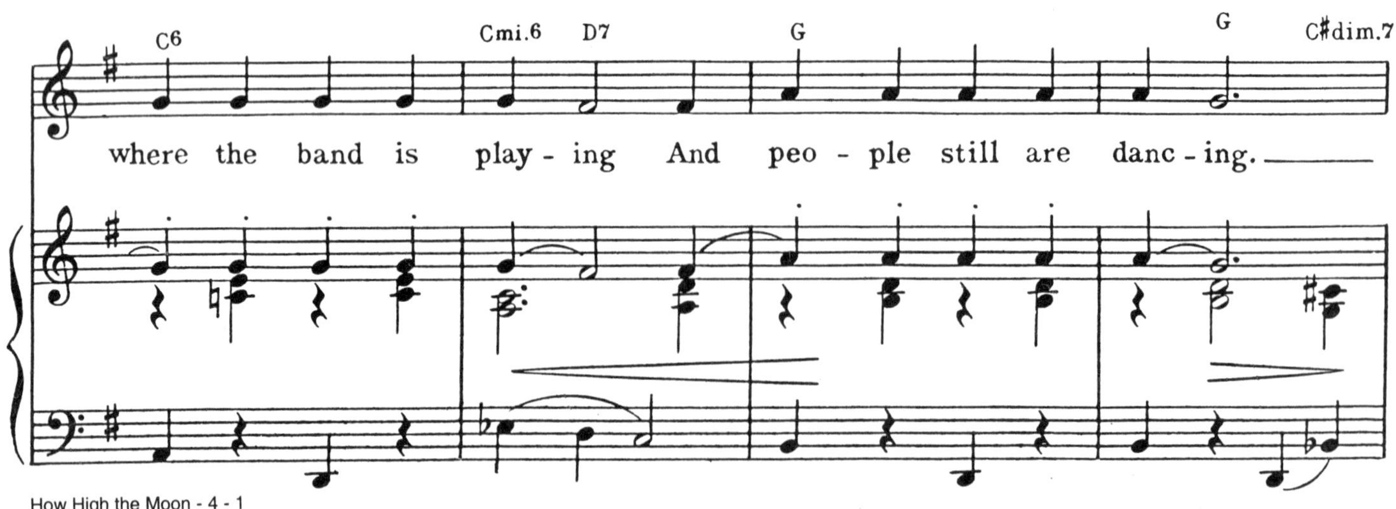

Am7
D7
G
F9
I know the moon still shines, But things that once were clear,
mf
B♭
Em7
Cm6
D7
Now I scarce - ly see or hear.
Refrain (Slowly, with expression)
A9
D7
Gmaj.7
G6
G
Gm7
C9
Some - where there's mu - sic, How faint the tune!
p - mf
C7
G9
C7(♭9)
Fmaj.7
F6
F
Some - where there's heav - en, How high the

Fm7
B♭9
B♭7
A♭
B♭7
E♭
E♭maj.7
moon! There is no moon a - bove When
Cm
D7
Gm
Cm6
love is far a - way too, Till it comes
G
Am
D7
G
Gm
Am7
D7
A9
D7
true That you love me as I love you. Some-where there's
mf
p
Gmaj.7
G6
G
Gm7
C9
C7
G9
C7(♭9)
mu - sic, It's where you are, Some-where there's

Fmaj.7
F6
F
Fm7
B♭9
B♭7
A♭
B♭7
heav - en, How near, how far! The dark - est
E♭
E♭maj.7
Cm
D7
G7
night would shine If you would come to me soon,
cresc.
C
Cm
G
Gm
Am7
D7
A9
D7♭9
Un - til you will, How still my heart, How high the
mf
p
1.G
D9+
G6
A9
D7
A9
D7
2. G
C6
Cm6
D7(G)
G6
moon! Some - where there's moon!
mf
mf

I CAN'T BEGIN TO TELL YOU

Words by
MACK GORDON

Music by
JAMES V. MONACO

Broadly
C Cmaj7 Gm6 A7 A+ Am7 Dm A7 Dm D9
I can't be-gin to tell you, how much you mean to me. My
pmf
G7 F6 F+ G7 C Edim Dm F G7 C Cmaj7
world will end if ev-er we were through. I can't be-gin to
Gm6 A7 Dm A7 Dm Am Dm D7 D9 G7 Em D
tell you how hap-py I would be, if I could speak my
G9 Em G7 C Ab7 Bb Fm C Dm6
mind like oth-ers do. I make such pret-ty

E7
A7
G6
Cdim
A7
A9
Bm
B♭m
D9
speech-es, when - ev - er we're a - part. But, when you're near, the
Bm
E♭m6
D+
Dm
G7
G9
F
Gdim
G7
C
Cmaj7
words I choose re - fuse to leave my heart. So, take the sweet - est
Gm6
A7
A+
Am7
Dm
A7
Dm
Dm6
Cdim
C
Cdim
phras-es the world has ev - er known, and make be - lieve I've
Dm7
Em
G7
1. C
Em7
Am
Cm7
Dm
F
G7
2. C
Am6
Fm
C
said them all to you. I you.

I COULDN'T SLEEP A WINK LAST NIGHT

I Couldn't Sleep a Wink Last Night - 3 - 1

Cm7
F7
F+
B♭
G7/B
Bdim7
F/C
C7sus
C7
thought of all the fool - ish things we said, and then, I just could - n't wait till I could
Slowly with much expression
Chorus:
F7
B♭
D7/A
A♭7(♭5)
see you a - gain. I could - n't sleep a wink last night be -
p – mf
G9
Dm7
G7
Gm7/C
C9
F7
cause we had that sil - ly fight. I thought my heart would break, the
B♭
Gm7
Gm7/C
C13
F7
whole night through. I knew that you'd be sor - ry, and I'm sor - ry too. I

B♭ D7/A A♭7(♭5) G9 Dm7 G7
did - n't have my fa - v'rite dream, the one in which I hold you
Gm7/C C9 F7 B♭ Gm7
tight. I had to call you up this morn - ing, to see if
Cm7 D7(♯5) D7 G7(♯5 ♭9) Cm7 F7
ev' - ry - thing was still all right. Yes, I had to call you up this
mf
Dm7 Gm7 Bdim7 C7 F13 F7(♭9) 1. B♭ Gm7 E♭m/G♭ F7 2. B♭
morn - ing, 'cause I could - n't sleep a wink last night. I night.
rit. mf

I COULD WRITE A BOOK

Words by
LORENZ HART

Music by
RICHARD RODGERS

Gm7
C7
Fmaj7
Em7
A7
But my bus - y mind is burn - ing to use what learn - ing I've got,
D7
G
G7
Dm7
G7
I won't waste an - y time, I'll strike while the i - ron is hot.
REFRAIN slowly, with expression
C
G7
C
If they asked me I could write a book,
p
G7
C
G7
C
C♯dim
— A - bout the way you walk and whis - per and

Dm7
G7
F
G7
C
A♭7
Dm7
G7
look, I could write a pre - face on
più espress.
C
F♯dim
G
C
F♯dim
G
E♭7
Am7
D7
how we met, so the world would nev - er for -
G
Dm7
G7
C
G7
get, And the sim - ple se - cret of the
mf
p
C
G7
C
G7
plot is just to tell them that I

C
C♯dim
Dm7
G7
F
G7
love you a lot, Then the
più espress.
C
A♭7
Dm7
G7
Gm7
C7
world dis - cov - ers as my book
F
Dm
C
C+
Dm7
G7
ends, How to make two lov - ers of
1. C
Dm7
G7
2. C
F
C
friends. If they friends.
mf
mf

I DIDN'T KNOW WHAT TIME IT WAS

Words by
LORENZ HART

Music by
RICHARD RODGERS

G
B7
C+7
E7
My im - ag - i - na - ry sleeve.
And now I
A7♭5
D9
C6
G
C6
G
know I was na - ive!
mf
p
REFRAIN
F♯m7
B7
Slowly and tenderly
Em
F♯m7
B7
I did - n't know what time it was, Then I met
p
A
Am
Em
Bm
C
Bm
you. Oh, what a love - ly time it was, How sub - lime it was,

Am Dm7 D7 F♯m7 B7 Em F♯m7 B7
too! I didn't know what day it was. You held my
A Am Em Bm C Bm
hand, Warm like the month of May it was And I'll say it was
Am7 F6 D7 G Am B7
grand. Grand to be a - live, to be young, to be
mf più espr.
Am B7 Em C D7 Gmaj7
mad, to be yours a - lone! Grand to see your face, feel your touch, hear your

Em7
A7
Am
Dm7
D7
F♯m7
B7
Em
voice say I'm all your own!
I ___ did - n't know what year it was.
p
F♯m7
B7
A
Am
Em
Bm
Life ___ was no prize.
I ___ want - ed love and here it was
C
Bm
Am7
Cm6
G
B7
C6
D7
C6
Shin - ing out of your eyes.
I'm wise ___ and I know what time it is
mf
1. G
Em6
D7
2. G
now!
now! ___
mf
f
Ped.
*

I LOVE YOU

Words and Music by
COLE PORTER

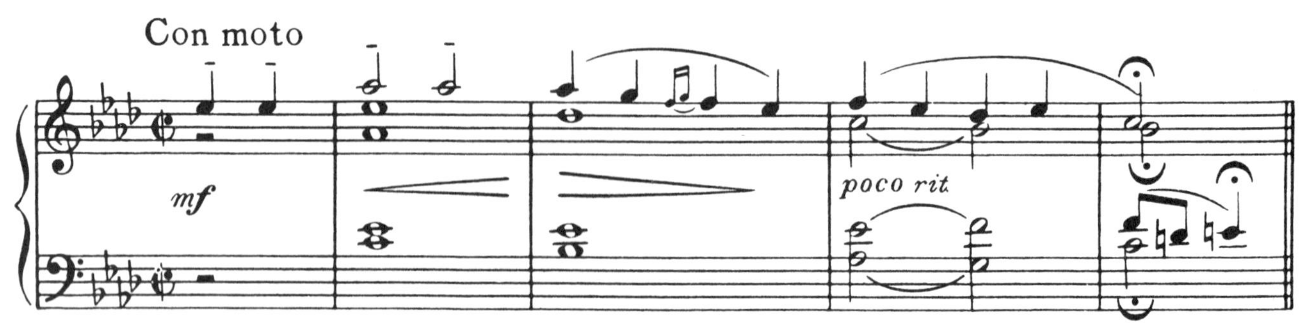

F
un pochettino più mosso
B♭m
F6
Fmaj. 7
F7
las, just an am - a - teur am I And so I'll
B♭
E♭m
B♭+
Gm
D7
not be sur - prised, my dear If you
mf
G7
F dim.
F
calmato
smile and po - lite - ly pass it by When this, my
più mosso
pp
G7
Gm7
C7
F
(four beats)
first love song, you hear
rit
a tempo

Refrain (in warm movement)
B♭m6
C7
F dim.
F
"I love you"
Hums the A - pril breeze
p-mf
Gm7
C7
"I love you"
echo the
3
F
D7
B♭m6
hills.
"I love you"
C7
F dim.
F
the gold - en dawn a - grees
As once

A
E7
A7
more she sees daf - fo - dils
poco a poco cresc.
Gm7
appassionato
C7
It's spring a - gain
And birds on the
f
F
Cm6
wing a - gain
start to sing a - gain
D7
Cm
D7
G7
C7
The old mel - o - die
"I

B♭m6
Tempo I
C7
Fdim.
F
F7
D7
love you" That's the song of songs, And it
G7
C7
1. F
Fdim.
C7(sus. 4)
C7
all be-longs to you and me. I
mf
2. F
B♭
F
B♭m
me And it all be - longs to you and
p
delicato
poco sostenuto
F
me.
p
pp

I WISH YOU LOVE

(Que Reste-T-il De Nos Amours?)

English Lyric by
ALBERT A. BEACH

Music and Original Lyric by
CHARLES TRENET

*Chord names and diagrams for guitar.

Ebm6
Cb7
Abm6
Bb7
I sin - cere ly want to - say:
Et je pense aux jours loin - tains.
Refrain
Edim
Fm7
Bb7
Fm7
Bb
Ebmaj.7
Eb6
Ebmaj.7
Eb6
I wish you blue - birds in the Spring, To give your heart a song to sing; And then a
Que res - te - t-il de nos a - mours, Que res - te - t-il de ces beaux jours, U - ne pho -
mp-mf
Fm7
Bb7
Eb6
Edim
Fm7
Bb7
kiss, but more than this I WISH YOU LOVE. And in Ju - ly, a lem - on -
to, vieil - le pho - to de ma jeu - nesse. Que res - te - t-il des bil - lets
Fm7
Bb7
Ebmaj.7
Eb6
Ebmaj.7
Eb6
Fm7
Bb7
ade, To cool you in some leaf - y glade; I wish you health and more than wealth, I WISH YOU
doux Des mois d'A - vril, des ren - dez - vous, Un sou - ve - nir qui me pour suit sans

Eb7 Ebdim Eb7 Ab Abm6 Eb Bbm6
LOVE. My break-ing heart and I a - gree That you and I could nev - er
cesse. Bon-heur fa - né Che-veux au vent, Bai - sers vo - lés, Rê - ves mou-
C7 Fm F9 Bb7 Ebm6 Bbdim Bb7 Edim
be, So with my best, my ver - y best, I set you free. I wish you
vants, Que res - te - t-il de tout ce - la Di - tes - le moi? Un p'tit vil-
Fm7 Bb7 Fm7 Bb7 Ebmaj.7 Eb6 Ebmaj.7 Eb6 Fm7
shel - ter from the storm, A co - zy fire to keep you warm; But most of all, when snow-flakes
lage, Un vieux clo - cher, Un pa - y - sage Si bien ca - ché Et dans un nuage le cher vi -
1. Bb7 Eb Edim 2. Bb7 Eb
fall, I WISH YOU LOVE. I wish you fall, I WISH YOU LOVE.
sage De mon pas - sé. Que res - te - sage De mon pas - sé.
mf

I'LL REMEMBER APRIL

Words and Music by
DON RAYE, GENE DE PAUL
and PAT JOHNSTON

G6
Cm7
F7
B♭maj7
B♭6
I'll be con - tent you loved me once in A - pril. Your
mp
Cm7
F7
B♭maj7
B♭6
Am7
lips were warm and love and Spring were new. But I'm not a - fraid of
3
f
D7
Gmaj7
G6
F♯m7
B9
Au - tumn and her sor - row, for I'll Re - mem - ber A - pril and
mf
Emaj7
E6
Am7
D7
G
G6
Gmaj7
you. The fire will dwin - dle in - to glow - ing
mp

G6
Gm7
Gm6
Gm7
Gm6
ash - es, for flames and love live such a lit - tle while. I
Cm6
D7
F9
E9
E7
won't for - get, but I won't be lone - ly, I'll Re -
mf
Am7
D7-9
G
G6
Gmaj7
mem - ber A - pril, and I'll smile.
G6
G
G6
G
smile.
p
pp
L.H.

I'VE GOT A GAL IN KALAMAZOO

Words by
MACK GORDON

Music by
HARRY WARREN

Eb
Fm7
Eb
Edim
Fm7
Bb7
my, how she grew; I liked her looks, when I car-
Fm7
Bb7
Eb
Eb7
Ab
Eb
ried her books in Kal-a-ma-zoo, zoo, zoo, zoo, zoo. I'm gon-na
G7-9
C7-9
Bbm6
send a wire, hop-pin' on a fly-er, leav-in' to-day.
C7
F7-9
Am I dream-in'; I can hear her scream-in', "Hy-

Eb
Ebdim
Fm7
F9
F7-5
Eb7
Coda
G7
C7
a Mis - ter Jack-son" ev - 'ry-thing's O
hur - ry-ing to.
F9
Eb7
Eb
Eb7
Ab
Abm
Eb7
I'm goin' to Mich - i - gan to see the sweet - est gal in Kal - a - ma -
Eb
Eb7
Ab
Eb7
Eb
Eb7
1.
2.
zoo.
zoo, zoo, zoo, zoo,
Ab
Eb
Ebdim
Eb7
Eb
zoo! Kal - a - ma - zoo!
f

IT CAN'T BE WRONG

Words by
KIM GANNON

Music by
MAX STEINER

Am7
B7
Dm6
E7
Here in your arms this way,
Un-der this star - ry sky?
If it is
Am7
D7
Gma7
Em7
Am7
wrong,
Then why were you sent to me,
Why am I con - tent to be
F7
D7
G
With you for - ev - - er?
So
when I need you so
F6
E7
+5
Am7
much
and I have wait - ed so long,
It must be right,
D7-9
Eb7
D7
1. G
Am7
D7-9
2. G
IT CAN'T BE WRONG.
WRONG.

JUKE BOX SATURDAY NIGHT

Cmi.7
F7
Cmi.7
F7
B♭
Faug.
B♭
They put noth - in' past us, — Me and hon - ey lamb, —
Dmi.7
G7
Dmi.7
G7
C7
Gmi.7
C7
Mak - ing one — coke last us — Till it's time to scram; —
F
F7
Mon - ey, we real - ly don't need that, — We make out — all right,
B♭
F
Fdim.
Gmi.7
Ami.
F
Gmi.7
C7
F
Let - tin' the oth - er guy feed — that — JUKE BOX SATURDAY NIGHT. NIGHT. —

IT NEVER ENTERED MY MIND

Words by
LORENZ HART

Music by
RICHARD RODGERS

A7
D7
G7
walk in a daze now, I never go to shows at night, But just to mat-in-ees now.
Gm7/C
C
Cm6
C9
I see the show and home I go.
poco rit.
Refrain (slowly, with warm expression)
F
Am
Once I laughed when I heard you say - ing That I'd be play - ing
p a tempo
sol - i - taire, Un-eas-y in my eas - y chair.

Gm7
E♭7
C7
F
Am
It nev - er en - tered my mind.
Once you told me
mf
p
I was mis - tak - en
That I'd a - wak - en
with the sun
And or - der or - ange juice for one,
It nev - er en - tered my mind.
F6/A
Fmaj7
F6
You have what I lack my - self,
mp

C7 F C7 F Ab°7 C7 Gm7 Am
And now I e-ven have to scratch my back my-self,
mf marcato
Bb Am C7 F Am F Am F Am
Once you warned me That if you scorned me, I'd sing the maid-en's
mp
F Am F Am Am7-5 D7+5 D7 Gm C7
pray'r a-gain And wish that you were there a-gain To get in-to my
mf
F Db6 C7 F6 1. G7 C7 2.
hair a-gain, It nev-er en-tered my mind.
mf
p
Ped.

VERSE

I don't care if there's powder on my nose.
I don't care if my hairdo is in place.
I've lost the very meaning of repose.
I never put a mudpack on my face.
Oh, who'd have thought
That I'd walk in a daze now?
I never go to shows at night,
But just to matinees now.
I see the show
And home I go.

REFRAIN 1

Once I laughed when I heard you saying
That I'd be playing solitaire,
Uneasy in my easy chair.
It never entered my mind.
Once you told me I was mistaken,
That I'd awaken with the sun
And order orange juice for one.
It never entered my mind.
You have what I lack myself,
And now I even have to scratch my back myself.
Once you warned me that if you scorned me
I'd sing the maiden's prayer again
And wish that you were there again
To get into my hair again.
It never entered my mind.

REFRAIN 2

Once you said in your funny lingo
I'd sit at bingo day and night
And never get the numbers right.
It never entered my mind.
Once you told me I'd stay up Sunday
To read the Monday-morning dirt
And find you're merging with some skirt.
It never entered my mind.
Life is not so sweet alone.*
The man who came to dinner lets me eat alone.
I confess it - I didn't guess it,
That I would sit and mope again
And all the while I'd hope again
To see my darling dope again.
It never entered my mind!

---

*Earlier version of refrain 2, lines 9-10:
You were my barometer,
And now my only friend is my thermometer.

LA VIE EN ROSE

Original French Words by
EDITH PIAF
English Words by
MACK DAVID

Music by
LOUIGUY

CHORUS Slowly with much expression
C
Cmaj7
C6
Hold me close and hold me fast, The mag - ic spell you
Quand il me prend dans ses bras Il me par - le tout
a tempo
mp - mf
C
Dm7
G7
Dm7
G7
cast, This is LA VIE EN ROSE.
bas, Je vois la vie en ro - se.
When you kiss me heav - en
Il me dit des mots d'a -
G7
Dm7
G7
C
F#m6
Dm7
G7
sighs, And tho' I close my eyes I see LA VIE EN ROSE.
mour, Des mots de tous les jours, Et ca m'fait quel - que cho - se.
C
Cmaj7
C6
When you press me to your heart I'm in a world a -
Il est en - tré dans mon cœur U - ne part de bon -

C
C7
F
Fm
part, A world where ros - es bloom; And when you speak An - gels
heur Dont je con - nais la cause. C'est lui pour moi. Moi pour
C
C
Eb
Dm7
G7-9
ten.
sing from a - bove; Ev - 'ry day words seem to turn in - to love songs.
lui, dans la vie, Il me l'a dit, l'a ju - ré pour la vi - e.
ten.
C
Cmaj7
C6
Give your heart and soul to me And life will al - ways
Et dès que je l'a - per - çois A - lors je sens en
Dm7
G7
1.
C
Ab9
4fr
Dm7
G7
2. C
Dm7
C
be LA VIE EN ROSE. ROSE.
moi Mon coeur qui bat. bat.
p
rall.

LEAP FROG

Words and Music by
LEO CORDAY and JOE GARLAND

C
1
2
leap frog.
leap frog.
Each day a
You just
Ab9
G9
leap and look for brand new charms. If you must jump, jump in my arms. You hold
C6
Dm7
me tight then hop from sight and that
G7
G7+5
D.S. al Coda
ain't right. You say you
CODA
C
C9#11
leap frog.

LOST IN THE STARS

Lyrics by
MAXWELL ANDERSON

Music by
KURT WEILL

G
Edim7
D7
G
E7
Lord God hunt - ed through the wide night air for the lit - tle dark star on the
Am
Cm
G/B
C
G/D
wind down_ there. And he stat - ed and prom-ised he'd take spe - cial care so it
Em7(♭5)/B♭
Am7(♭5)
D7
G
Cm7
E♭7
would - n't get lost a - gain. Now a man don't mind if the
B♭/D
Gm7
E♭m/G♭
Gm
stars grow dim and the clouds blow o - ver and dark - en him, so

Cm7 Eb7/Db Bb/D Gm Ebm/Gb F7 F7(#5)
long as the Lord God's watch - ing o - ver them, keep - ing track how it all goes
E7 Eb7 D7 G Edim7 D7
on. But I've been walk - ing through the night and the day till my
mf
G E7 Am Cm G/B
eyes get wear - y and my head turns gray. And some - times it seems may - be
f
Cm6 G/B
God's gone a - way, for - get - ting the prom - ise that we

Cm6
D7
Am7/D
G
heard him say.
And we're lost out here in the stars,
mp
Em7
E♭7
G/D
C♯dim7
D
Am7/D
lit - tle stars, big stars, blow - ing through the night, and we're lost out
p
G
Em7
E♭7
G/D
Am
E7(♭9)
B♭dim7
here in the stars, lit - tle stars, big stars, blow - ing through the night,
f
D7
G
E♭7
G6
and we're lost out here in the stars.
dim.
p

LOVER MAN
(Oh, Where Can You Be?)

Words and Music by
JIMMY DAVIS, ROGER "RAM" RAMIREZ
and JIMMY SHERMAN

F9
B♭9
G9
C
Em7
E7+5
5 fr.
oh, what I've been miss - in',
lov - er man, oh, where can you be?
Am7
D7
Dm/A
D7
The night is cold,
and I'm so all a - lone.
(Inst.)
Dm7/G
G9
B♭/D
G7
I'd give my soul just to call you my own.
(Inst.)
C7-9
F9
Got a moon a - bove me,
there's no one to love me,
(Inst.)

B♭9
G9
C
Bm7-5
(Inst.)
lov - er man, oh, where can you be?
Em
Em+5
Am7
A7
I've heard it said that the thrill of ro - mance can
Dmaj7
A♭7-5
Gmaj7
F♯m7-5
Dm7
Dm+5
be like a heav - en - ly dream.
I go to bed
Gm7
3fr.
G7
Cmaj7
G♭7
Fmaj7
E7+5
5 fr.
with a pray'r that you'll make love to me,
strange as it seems.

Am7
D7
Am7
D7
G7
Dm7/G
Some-day we'll meet and you'll dry all my tears and whis-per sweet lit-tle
Dm7
G7
C7+9
things in my ears.
Hug-gin' and a kiss-in',
D. S. al Coda
F9
B♭9
G9
C
Em7
E7+5
To Coda
ooo, what I've been miss-ing; lov-er man, oh, where can you be?
Coda
B♭9
G9
C7+9
lov-er man, oh, where can you be?
rit.
a tempo
mp

THE LAST TIME I SAW PARIS

Words by
OSCAR HAMMERSTEIN II

Music by
JEROME KERN

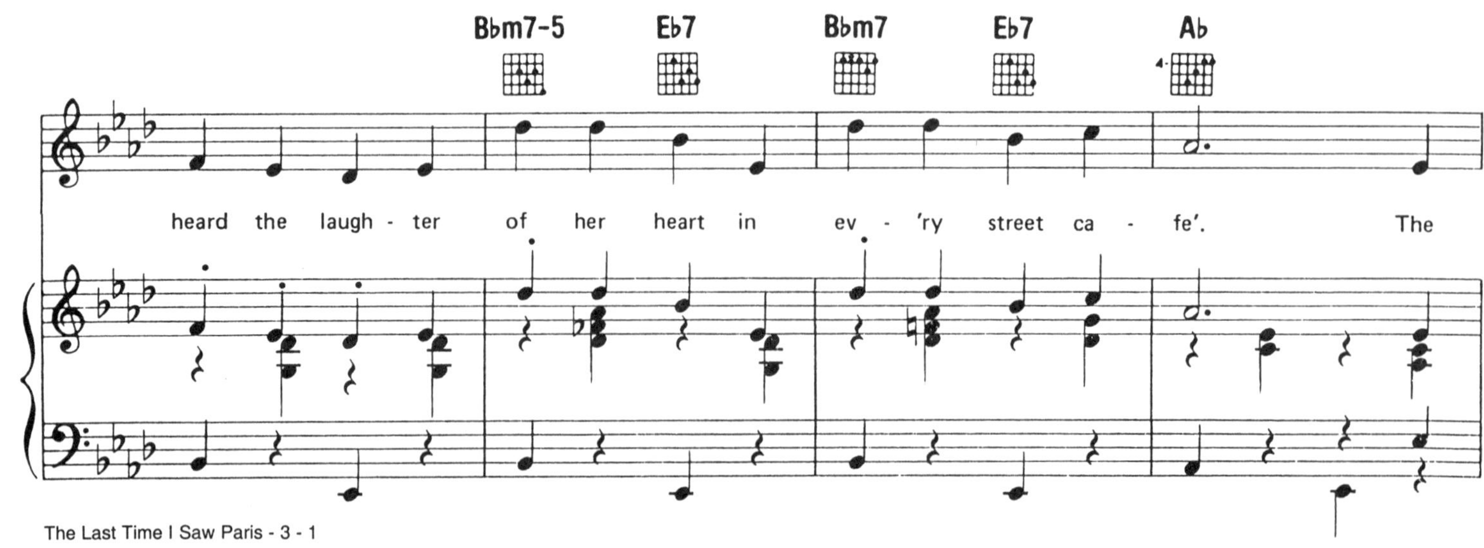

Eb7
last time I saw Par - is, Her trees were dressed for spring, And
Bbm7-5 Eb7 Bbm7 Eb7
lov - ers walked be - neath those trees, and birds found songs to
Ab Bb7 Eb Bb7
Brightly
sing. I dodged the same old tax - i - cabs that I had dodged for
Eb C7 F Bbm7
nostalgically
years; The cho - rus of their squeak - y horns was mu - sic to my

Eb7
Ab
ears The last time I saw Par - is Her heart was warm and
a tempo
Eb7
Bbm7
Eb7
Cm7-5
F7
Bbm7
deliberato
3
gay. No mat - ter how they change her I'll re - mem - ber her
ritardando
col canto
Eb7
1 Ab
Eb7
that way.
dim.
a tempo
mf
Ab
Eb7
2 Ab
The way.
dim. e rit.
p
Ped.
*

MOONLIGHT IN VERMONT

Words by
JOHN BLACKBURN

Music by
KARL SUESSDORF

Moonlight in Vermont - 5 - 1

D♭6/9 B♭m7 G♭m(maj7) G♭m7 G♭m6 N.C. E♭m9 E♭m7/A♭ D♭6/9
ski trails down the moun-tain-side, L.R.: snow-light in Ver-mont.
Gm9 C13(♭5/♭9) Fmaj9 D7(♭9) Gm9 C7(♯5/♯9)
Tel-e-graph ca-bles, they sing down the high-way and trav-el each bend in the
mp
Fmaj 7 A♭m9 D♭7(♭9) G♭maj9 E♭7(♭9)
road. F.S.: Peo-ple who meet in this ro-man-tic set-ting are
A♭m9 D♭7(♯5/♯9) G♭maj9 A♭13(♭9) D♭6/9
(F.S.) so hyp-no-tized by the love-ly eve-ning
L.R.: Eve-ning sum-mer

Ebm9
Ab13(b9)
Db6/9
Bbm7
Gbm(maj7)
Cb9
— summer breeze,
the sweet warb-ling
of a mea-dow-lark,
breeze,
warb - ling
of a mea-dow-lark,
Ebm7
Ab13sus
Db6/9
C7(#5 #9)
F13(b9)
Bb6/9
moon-light
in Ver-mont.
moon-light
in Ver-mont.
Ic - y fin-ger
Cm9
F13(b9)
Bbmaj9
Gm7
Cm9(b5)
Dbm9
Cm9
Cm7/F
(L.R.) waves,
ski trails
on a moun-tain-side,
snow-light
in Ver-

B♭6/9
C13sus
C13(♭5/♭9)
Fmaj9
D7(♭9)
mont.
F.S.: Tel-e-graph ca-bles, how they sing down the high-way,
Gm9
C7(♯5/♯9)
Fmaj 7
A♭m9
D♭7(♭9)
as they make ev-'ry bend in the road.
Peo-ple who meet
L.R.: Ooh,
cresc.
G♭maj9
A13
A♭m7
D♭7(♯5)
G♭maj 7
E9
in this ro-man-tic set-ting are so hyp-no-tized by the love-ly
are so hyp-no-tized by the love-ly
molto rit.
mf

E♭maj9
Fm9
B♭13(♭9)
E♭maj 7
B♭/C Cm7
eve - ning summer breeze,
the sweet warb - ling of the
eve - ning summer breeze,
dim.
mp
D♭13(♯11)
D♭9 D♭7sus D♭9
Fm11
Fm7/B♭
E♭6/9
Cm7
Fm11
Fm7/B♭
mea-dow-lark,
moon-light in Ver-mont.
Snow-light in Ver-
moon-light in Ver-mont.
Snow-light in Ver-
dim.
p
E♭6/9
G♭13
Fm9
A♭/B♭
Emaj9
E♭maj9
mont.
Moon - light
in Ver - mont.
mont.
You and me and moon-light
in Ver - mont.
dim. e rit.
pp

MAIRZY DOATS

Words and Music by
JERRY LIVINGSTON,
MILTON DRAKE and AL HOFFMAN

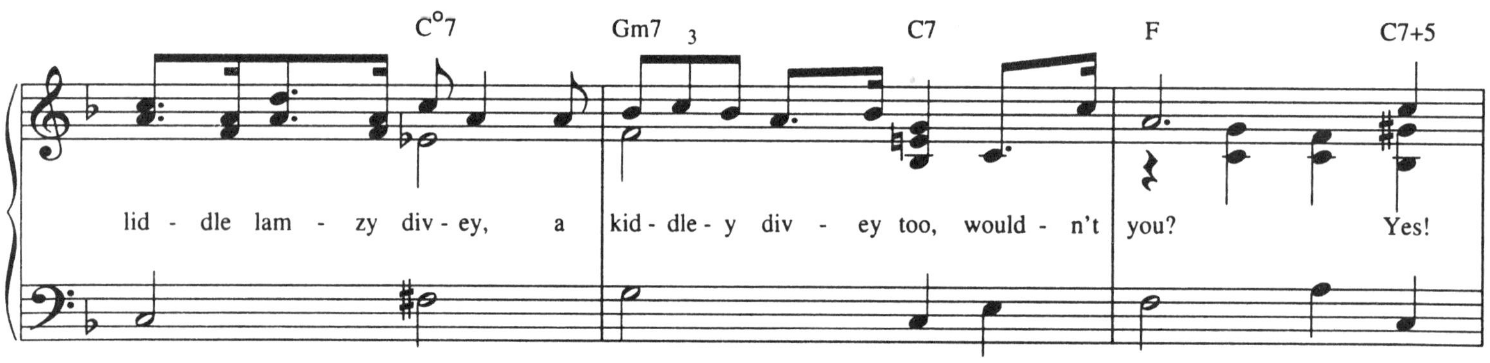

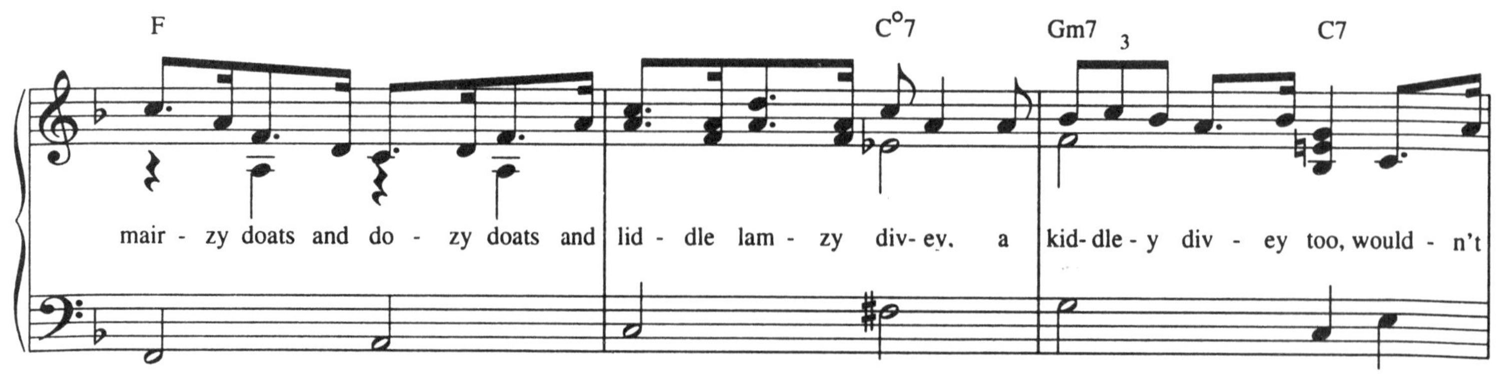

Mairzy Doats - 2 - 1

F
Cm7
F7
Cm7
F7
you? If the words sound queer and fun - ny to your ear, a
3
B♭
E°7
B♭
Dm7
G7
lit - tle bit jum - bled and jiv - ey, sing, "Mares eat oats and
Dm7
G7
C
Gm7
C7
does eat oats and lit - tle lambs eat i - vy." Oh!
F
C°7
Gm7
3
C7
Mair - zy doats and do - zy doats and lid - dle lam - zy div - ey, a kid - dle - y div - ey too, would - n't
F
C°7
Gm7
3
C7
F
you? A kid - dle - y div - ey too, would - n't you?

MOONLIGHT SERENADE

Moonlight Serenade - 2 - 1

B♭maj7 B♭m6 Em7 A7 Cm6 D7+5
Let us stray till break of day in love's val - ley of dreams, Just
mf
Dm6 E7 Dm6 E7 Cm6 D7 Gm7 C7-9
you and I, a sum - mer sky, a heav - en - ly breeze kiss - ing the trees. So
mp
F6 A♭dim Gm7 Cdim C7 C7+5
don't let me wait, come to me ten - der - ly in the June night, I
F Fmaj7 F7 D7 Gm
stand at your gate and I sing you a song in the moon - light, A
F Edim F Gm Gdim Gm C7 C7+5 F F6
love song, my dar - ling, a Moon - light Ser - e - nade.
rit. e dim.

THE MORE I SEE YOU

Words by
MACK GORDON

Music by
HARRY WARREN

Refrain, with feeling
Fm7
Ebdim
Eb
Bb7
Eb
Ebmaj7
Fm7
Bb7
Fm7
Ebdim
The more I see you, the more I want you. Some-how this
Eb
Bb7
Eb
Ebdim
Fm7
Bb7
Fm7
Bb7
feel - ing just grows and grows. With ev - 'ry
Ebm
Eb
Dbm
Gb7
Cb
Abm7
Bb7+
sigh I be - come more mad a - bout you; more lost with -
Ebm
F9
Fm7
Bb7
Fm7
Eb
Fm7
Ebdim
out you, and so it goes. Can you im -

Eb Bb7 Eb Ebmaj7 Fm7 Bb7 Fm7 Ebdim
ag - ine how much I'll love you, the more I
Eb Bb7 Eb Bb+ Bbm7 Eb7 Bbm7 Eb7 Dbm Bbdim Ab 4th Fret
see you as years go by? I know the on - ly one for
Abm Eb C7 F7 Eb Fm7 Fdim
me can on - ly be you. My arms won't free you, my heart won't
1. Eb Fm7 Ebdim 2. Eb Ab9 Eb
try. The more I try.

MY SHIP

Lyrics by
IRA GERSHWIN

Music by
KURT WEILL

My Ship - 3 - 1

G7
C7
F
F♯dim
G7
C+
mil - lion pearls and ru - bies fill each bin, The
F
D7
Gm
A
Dm
G13
B♭/C
F
sun sits high in a sap - phire sky when my ship comes in. I can
mp
Gm7
Am
C7
Gm7
Am
C7
Gm7
C7
B♭m6
F
E7
wait the years till it ap - pears one fine day one spring, But the
mf
Am
D7
Am
Dm7
G7
Edim
G7
C7
pearls and such they won't mean much if there's miss - ing just one thing. I
p

F
D7
G7
C7
F
D7
Dm7
C+
do not care if that day ar - rives, That dream need nev - er be, If the
F
D7
Gm
A7
1 Dm
Gm
C7
F
Db7
C7
ship I sing does - n't al - so bring my own true love to me. My
ten.
ten.
2 Dm
C7
F
C7
F
Dm
Bb7
F
Bb
own true love to me, If the ship I sing does - n't al - so bring my
mf
F
Gm
Gm7-5
C7
F
Db7
F
own true love to me.
dim.
p
pp
Ped.

MY FOOLISH HEART

Words by
NED WASHINGTON

Music by
VICTOR YOUNG

Bb
Gm
Cm7
Adim
Bbmaj7
lips ___ are much too close to mine, Be - ware ___ My Fool-ish Heart But should ___ our ea-ger
Gm
Cm7
D7+5
D7
D7-5
D7
Gm
Gm7
lips com-bine Then let ___ the fire start For this time it is-n't fas-ci-
Gb9
Gb7
Bb
Dm7-5
G7
Cm7
na - tion, or a dream that will fade and fall a - part, It's love ___ this time, it's
F9
Cm7
F7-9
1
Bb
Gm7
Cm7
F7
2
Bb
Gm7
Cm7
Cb7
Bb6
love, My Fool - ish Heart. ___ The heart. ___
mp
rall.

MY HEART TELLS ME
(Should I Believe My Heart)

Words by
MACK GORDON

Music by
HARRY WARREN

F
C
G7
Caug
Ev - 'ry - thing, —
Do you mean what you are say - ing,
poco cresc
Am
D9
Dm7
Fm
Em
Gdim
or is this a lit - tle game you're play - ing? MY HEART TELLS ME I will
rall.
a tempo
Dm
Bbm
cry a - gain, —
Lips that kiss like yours could lie a - gain, —
Am7
Cdim
Cm
Gm
A7
If I'm fool e - nough to see this thru, Will I be sor - ry if I do, Should
poco cresc.
rall.
a tempo
Ddim
I be - lieve my heart or you? —
you? —
p
pp

MY WILD IRISH ROSE

By
CHAUNCEY OLCOTT

G7
C
E7
Am
Em7
Am
giv - en to me by a girl that I know; Since we've met, faith, I've
glan - ces are shy when — e'er I pass by The bow - er where
D7
G7
C
C+
known no re - pose, She is dear - er by far than the
my true love grows. And my one wish has been that some
Dm7
C
G7
Fm
G7
C
F
C
world's bright-est star, And I call her my wild I - rish rose.
day I may win The — heart of my wild I - rish rose.
rit.
C
Fm
C
Dm7
C
Refrain: (with much expression)
My wild I - rish rose, The sweet-est flow'r that grows,
mf
a tempo

C#o G7 C C#o G7 C D7
— You may search ev-'ry-where, but none can com-pare With my wild
G7 C Fm C
I - rish rose. My wild I - rish rose,
mf
Dm7 C C#o G7
— The dear-est flow'r that grows, And some day for my
C C#o G7 C F C D7 G7 C
rit.
sake, she may let me take The bloom from my wild I - rish rose.
rit.

NANCY
(With the Laughing Face)

Words by
PHIL SILVERS

Music by
JAMES VAN HEUSEN

Nancy - 3 - 1

1.
Cm
Gm7
F7
Fm7
B♭7
Gdim
2.
A♭m
NAN-CY with the laugh-ing face.
She takes the
NAN-CY with the laugh-ing face.
E♭
G7
Cm
Do you ev-er hear mis-sion bells ring-ing?
What a won-der-ful treat to come home to,
E♭+
Cm7
Well, she'll give you the ver-y same glow.
When the long day has drawn to a close.
F9
F9 (add C♭ no C)
A♭m
E♭
When she speaks you would think it was sing-
There's the pat-ter of feet to come home

Fm7
B♭7
G7+
Cm
Cm7
F7
Fm7
B♭7
Gdim
– ing, Just hear her say, "Hel - lo." I swear to
— to, And NAN - CY gave me those. Keep Bet - ty
Fm7
B♭7
E♭
good-ness you can't — re - sist her, Sor - ry for you — she
Gra - ble, La - mour, — and Tur - ner, She makes my heart — a
D
F♯m
Fm
has no sis - ter.
char - coal bur - ner.
No one could ev - er re - place —
Fm6
G7
Cm
A♭m
E♭
A♭6
E♭6
— my NAN - CY with the laugh - ing face. —
8vb

NEAR YOU

Words by
KERMIT GOELL

Music by
FRANCIS CRAIG

C7
just two lips a - way. If my hours could be spent,
F
near you, I'd be
A7
more than con - tent
Dm
near you.
F7
Bb
Make my like worth - while,
Eb7
E7
by
F
tell - ing me that
D7
I'll spend the
C
rest of my days
E
F
near you.

NEW YORK, NEW YORK

Words by
BETTY COMDEN and ADOLPH GREEN

Music by
LEONARD BERNSTEIN

Eb
Cdim
Bb7
Eb
Bb7
in it be-neath the Broad-way lights; But we've hair on our chest, so what we
an-y, and we have just one day; Got-ta see the whole town right from Yonk-
hat-tan when you have just one day; Got-ta pick up a date, may-be sev-
Eb6
Cdim
Bb7
Eb
like the best are the nights, sights, lights, nights. NEW
-ers on down to the bay in just one day. NEW
-en or eight on your way, in just one day. NEW
G6
D7
G6
YORK, NEW YORK, a hell-uv-a town, The Bronx is up but the
YORK, NEW YORK, a vis-it-or's place, Where no one lives on ac-
YORK, NEW YORK, a hell-uv-a town, The Bronx is up but the

D7
G6
D7
G6
F7
1. 2.
Bb
Bat-ter-y's down, And peo-ple ride in a hole in the ground; NEW YORK, NEW YORK,
count of the pace, But sev-en mil-lion are scream-ing for space; NEW YORK, NEW YORK
Bat-ter-y's down, And peo-ple ride in a hole in the ground; NEW
D7
G
G7
Eb6
Bbm7
Eb6
Bbmaj7
Bbm7
It's a hell-uv-a town!
is a vis-it-or's place!
Last time
Bb
D7
YORK, NEW YORK,
It's a hell-uv-a town!
f
G
C7
G6
Eb
D9
G
ff

THE OLD LAMPLIGHTER

Words by
CHARLES TOBIAS

Music by
NAT SIMON

F
A7
Dm
F7/C
B♭
Bdim
whit - er be - neath the can - dle glow, The old lamp -
bright - er wher - ev - er he would go, The old lamp -
F/C
B♭/D
F/C
C7
F
n.c.
light - er of long, long a - go. You'd hear the
light - er of long, long a - go. Now if you
F
F6
F
F6
F
F6
To Coda
pat - ter of his feet as he came tod - dling down the street, His smile would hide a lone - ly heart you
look up at the sky you'll un - der - stand the rea - son why The lit - tle stars at night are all a -
F
Gm
Gm6
Gm
Gm6
see. If there were sweet - hearts in the park he'd pass a lamp and leave it dark Re -

Gm Gm6 Gm F F6
mem - ber - ing the days that used to be. For he re - calls when dreams were new, he loved some -
F F6 F B♭/D C7 F
D.S. al Coda
n.c.
one who loved him too Who walks with him a - lone in mem - o - ry. He made the
CODA
F F F6
n.c.
glow. He turns them on when night is here, he turns them
F F6 F B♭/D C7 F
off when dawn is here, The lit - tle man we loved of long a - go.
8va

OH! WHAT IT SEEMED TO BE

Words and Music by
BENNIE BENJAMIN, GEORGE DAVID WEISS
and FRANKIE CARLE

Eb Adim Bb7
just a ride on a train, that's all _ that it was, but OH, WHAT IT SEEMED TO BE! It was
mp
Ddim Eb Eb7
like a trip to the stars, to Ve-nus and Mars,'Cause you were on the train with me. ___ And when I
Broadly
Ab Eb Cm7 Fm Bb7 Eb Eb7
kissed you, ___ dar - ling, ___ It was more than just a thrill for me; ___ It was the
Ab Eb Bbm C7 F7 Fm7 Bb7
prom-ise, ___ dar - ling, ___ Of the things that fate had willed for me. It was
Eb Adim Bb7
just a wed-ding in June, that's all _ that it was, but OH, WHAT IT SEEMED TO BE! It was
mp
Ddim 1.Eb Bb7 2Eb
like a roy - al af-fair with ev-'ry-one there,'Cause you said "Yes, I do," to me. _ It was _

ON GREEN DOLPHIN STREET

Lyrics by
NED WASHINGTON

Music by
BRONISLAU KAPER

Db C Dmi7 G7 G7aug 9
plan-ning to stay. Green Dol-phin Street sup-plied the
C Fmi7 Bb7 Bb7aug 9 Eb G7
set-ting The set-ting for nights be-yond for-get-ting. And
C Cmi7 D7 Db
through these mo-ments a-part mem-ries live in my
C Dmi7 G7 E7 Ami D7 D7-9
heart. When I re-call the love I found on, I could kiss the
C Gdim Dmi7 G7 - G7+ 1 C Dmi7 G7 2 C F Fm6 C
ground On Green Dol-phin Street. Street.

ON THE ATCHISON, TOPEKA AND THE SANTA FE

Lyric by
JOHNNY MERCER

Music by
HARRY WARREN

On the Atchison, Topeka and the Santa Fe - 3 - 1

C G7 C
ol' smoke ris - in' 'round the bend, I reck - on that she knows she's gon - na
F
C F6 C G+ C G7 C G7 C G#dim Am Ab7
meet a friend, Folks a - round these parts get the time o' day From The
C G#dim Am Dm7 G7 C Eb7 Ab6
Atch - i - son, To - pe - ka And The San - ta Fe. Here she comes! Ooh,
Ebmaj7 Ab6 Ab Ebmaj7 Ab6 Eb
Ooh, Ooh, Hey, Jim! yuh bet - ter git the rig!
Ab6 Ebmaj7 Ab6
Ooh, Ooh, Ooh, She's

Cm Ebmaj7 Fm6 Cm7 Fm Abmaj7 Fm6 G7 C G7 C
got a list o' pas-sen-gers that's pret-ty big And they'll all want lifts to
Brown's Ho-tel, 'Cause lots o' them been trav-el-in' for quite a spell, All the
F C F6 C G+
C G7 Cmaj7 C7 F6 C G#dim Am Dm7
way from Phil-a-del-phi-ay, On The Atch-i-son, To-pe-ka And The
1 G7 C G7 2 G7 C
San-ta Fe. Do yuh San-ta Fe.
G9 (addE)
(Single notes)
C D E G E D C A G
C B C Fdim Cdim C

PENNSYLVANIA 6-5000

Lyric by
CARL SIGMAN

Music by
JERRY GRAY

G
C9
Chorus, Moderately (with a swing)
Num-bers I've got by the doz - en
ev-'ry-one's un-cle and
p-mf
Ddim
Am7
D7
cous - in
But I can't live with-out buzz - in'
Guitar Tacet
(spoken)
D7+
Penn-syl-van-ia Six, Five Thou-sand
I've got a sweet-y I know there
Some-one who sets me a - glow there
Gives me the sweet-est "hel -
lo there"
Penn-syl-van-ia Six, Five Thou-sand
Am
B7+
B7
We don't say "how are

Em Am B7+ B7 Em E7-5
— you" and ver - y sel - dom ask — "what's new?" — In-
A7 add 6 A7 D C7 B7 E9 A7
stead we start and end each call — with "ba - by con - fi - den - tial - ly I —
D7 Eb9 D7 G C9
— love you" — may - be it sounds a bit fun - ny —
G Ddim Am7 D7
When I'm a - way from my hon - ey — here's what I do with my mon - ey —
1. G D+ 2. G G6
Guitar Tacet
(spoken)
Penn-syl-van-ia Six, Five Thou-sand
Penn-syl-van-ia Six, Five Thou-sand

PUT THE BLAME ON MAME

Words and Music by
DORIS FISHER and
ALLAN ROBERTS

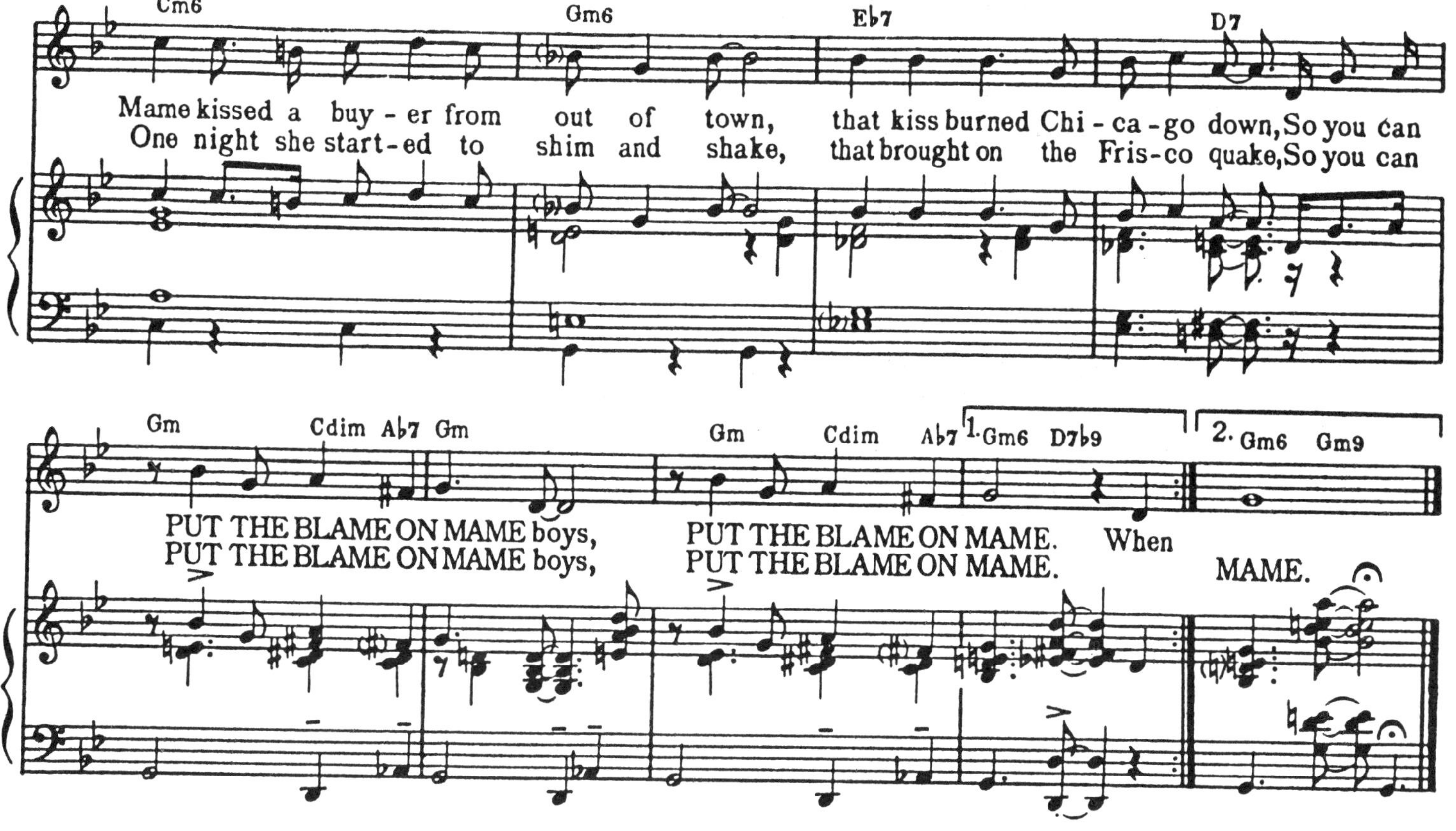

Extra Choruses

When they had the gold rush folks started running to Cal-i-for-ni-ay,
They all had dreams of making a million bucks a day.
That's the story that went around but here's the real low down:
"Put The Blame On Mame," boys, "Put The Blame On Mame."
She caused the gold rush, It's my belief,
Diggin' gold from some guys teeth.
So you can "Put The Blame On Mame," boys, "Put The Blame On Mame,"

Remember the blizzard back in Manhattan, in eighteen-eighty-six?
They say the traffic was tied up and folks were in a fix.
That's the story that went around but here's the real low down.
"Put The Blame On Mame," boys, "Put The Blame On Mame."
Mame gave a chump such an ice-cold no,
For seven days they shoveled snow.
So you can "Put The Blame On Mame," boys, "Put The Blame On Mame."

There was once a shootin' up in the Klondike when they got Dan Magrew
Folks were puttin' the blame on the lady known as "Lou."
That's the story that went around but here's the real low down:
"Put The Blame On Mame," boys, Put The Blame On Mame
Mame did a dance and she dropped her fan
That's the thing that murdered Dan
So you can "Put The Blame On Mame," boys, "Put The Blame On Mame."

PISTOL PACKIN' MAMA

Words and Music by
AL DEXTER

SATURDAY NIGHT IS THE LONELIEST NIGHT OF THE WEEK

Words by
SAMMY CAHN

Music by
JULE STYNE

F#dim
Gm
Adim
Bb
Gm7
night friends come to call
And Mon - day to Fri - day go fast
Cm9
F9
Bb7
Fm7
Gm
Fm7
Bb7
and an - oth - er week is past,
But
Eb
Bb7
Eb
Bb7
Eb
Bbm
Sat - ur - day Night is the lone - li - est night in the week,
mf
C7
Ebdim
C+
C7
Fm
Db7
Fm
Db7
I sing the song that I sang for the mem - 'ries I u - sual - ly seek

Fm
Abm
Bb7
Eb
G7
Un - til I hear you at the door
Cm
Em7
G7
Cm
Abm
Un - til you're in my arms once more
Eb
C7
Fm9
1
Eb
Fm7
Sat - ur - day Night is the lone - li - est night in the week.
Eb
Fm7
Bb+
2
Eb
Fm7
Eb
Ddim
Eb

RAG MOP

Words and Music by
JOHNNIE LEE WILLS and DEACON ANDERSON

Chorus–After 2nd and 5th Verses
F6
Bb7
Rag Mop!
Rag Mop!
Rag Mop!
F6
C7
Rag Mop!
Rag Mop!
F6
Bb
C11
F6
1,2,3 4
C7
D.S. and Repeat
R - A - G - G, M - O - P - P, Rag Mop!
5
F6
F
F7
Bb
Bbm
F
C11
F6
Mop! Mop!

'ROUND MIDNIGHT

Words by
BERNIE HANIGHEN

Music by
COOTIE WILLIAMS and THELONIOUS MONK

Ebm
Ebm/D
Ebm/Db
Cm7-5
Fm7-5
Fb9
It be - gins to tell 'round mid - night, 'round mid - night.
Ebm
Ebm/D
Cm7-5
Bm7(add C♯)
E7(add C♯)
Bbm7(add C)
Eb7(add C)
I do pret - ty well till af - ter sun - down.
Abm7
Db9
Fb7
Ebm9
Ab9
Sup - per - time, I'm feel - ing sad. But it
Cm7-5
F7+5-5
Cb9
Bb9
Fb7-5
real - ly gets bad 'round mid - night.

Ebm
Ebm/D
Ebm/Db
Cm7-5
Fm7-5
Fb9
Mem - 'ries al - ways start 'round mid - night, 'round mid - night.
Ebm
Ebm/D
Cm7-5
Bm7(add C#)
E7(add C#)
Bbm7(add C)
Eb7(add C)
Have - n't got the heart to stand those mem - 'ries,
Abm7
Db9
Fb7
Ebm9
Ab9
when my heart is still with you, and old
Cm7-5
F7-5
Cb9
Ab/Bb
Eb(add F)
mid - night knows it too.
When some

F7+5
Cb9
Bb9
Fb7-5
Ebm7
quar - rel we had needs mend - ing, does it
Cm7-5
F7+5
Cb9
Bb13
mean that our love is end - ing?
Abm7
Bb7+5
Cm7-5
F7+5
Bb13
Dar - ling, I need you; late - ly I find you're
Eb9+11
Db9+11
Abm7
Fm7-5
Bb7+5
Fb7
out of my arms and I'm out of my mind.

Ebm
Ebm/D
Ebm/Db
Cm7-5
Fm7-5
Fb9
Let our love take wing some mid - night, 'round mid - night.
Ebm
Ebm/D
Cm7-5
Bm7(add C#)
E7(add C#)
Bbm7(add C)
Eb7(add C)
Let the an - gels sing for your re - turn - ing.
Abm7
Db9
Fb7
Ebm9
Ab9
Let our love be safe and sound when old
Cm7-5
F7-5
Cb9
Ab/Bb
Eb(add F)
Tacet
mid - night comes a - round.

Cm7-5
Cb7
Cm7-5
Cb7
F#m7
B7
Am7
B7
D6/E
7fr
Fm7
Bb13+11
Ebm7
C#m9
F#9
3fr
Bm9
E9
Am9
5fr
Bb7-5
Eb6/9
5fr
rit.

RUM AND COCA-COLA

Lyric by
MOREY AMSTERDAM
Additional Lyrics by
AL STILLMAN

Music by
JERI SULLAVAN and PAUL BARON

Chorus, Moderately
C
Dm7
G7
Dm7
G7
Drink-in' Rum And Co-ca Co-la, Go down "Point Koo - mah-nah" Both moth-er and
daugh-ter Sing-in' for the Yan-kee dol - lar.
D9
G7
C
1
F
C
An - y
2
F
C
Drink-in' Rum And Co-ca Co-la,
Rum And Co-ca Co-la.
G7
C
mf

SOMEBODY LOVES ME

Words by
BALLARD MACDONALD and B.G. DeSYLVA
French version by EMELIA RENAUD

Music by
GEORGE GERSHWIN

Am7 D7 sus G D7 G7 Em Cm6 D7 Em Em6
Heav - en's pret - ty pro - gram for we've nev - er met; I'm
Bm Bm6 E7 Em7 A7 D7 D+
poco rit.
clutch - ing at straws, just be - cause I may meet her yet.
poco rit
Refrain
G (molto legato)
a tempo
p-f
Am7 Am D G
Some - bod - y loves me I won - der
p-f a tempo
C7 G C7 Am7 D7
who, I won - der who she can be; —

G
D7-9
G
Some - bod - y
Am7
Am
D7
G
A7
loves me I wish I knew,
Bm
C♯7-9
C♯m7
F♯7
Bm
Who can she be wor - ries me,
E7
Am
Dm6
Am
Dm6
For ev - 'ry girl who pass - es me I shout, Hey!

Am
Em7
A7
Em7
A7
may - be,
You were meant to be my lov - ing
D7
D+
G
Am7
Am
D7
ba - by;
Some - bod - y loves me
G
C7
G
Em
Am7
D7
I won - der who,
May - be it's
1. G
D7
2. G
Am
G
you.
you.
mf
rit. e dim.
fz

SPEAK LOW

Lyrics by
OGDEN NASH

Music by
KURT WEILL

B♭m
E♭9
B♭m
E♭9
low when you speak, love, Our mo-ment is
G9
C9
C7-9
F6
D7
Gm7
C+
swift, like ships a-drift, we're swept a-part too soon Speak
p
Gm9
C9
Gm9
C9
low dar-ling, speak low love is a
Gm9
C9
Gm9
C9
F6
D7
spark lost in the dark too soon, too soon, I

Bbm
Eb9
Bbm
Eb9
feel wher-ev-er I go that to mor-row is
G9
C9
C7-9
F
near, to-mor-row is here and al-ways too soon.
Fm7
Abm
4 fr.
Time is so old and love so brief,
mf più espr.
Ebmaj7
Fdim
E7
C+
Gm9
Love is pure gold and time a thief. We're late

C9 Gm9 C9 Gm9 C9
— dar-ling, we're late The cur-tain de-scends, ev'-ry-thing
Gm9 C7 F6 D B♭m
ends too soon, too soon I wait
Gm7-5 F B♭+ D7 G9 C9+5
— dar-ling, I wait Will you speak low to me, speak love to me and
espressivo
rall.
1. F D7 Gm7 C+ 2. F
soon. Speak soon.
mf
a tempo
L.H. p

A STRING OF PEARLS

Words by
EDDIE DeLANGE

Music by
JERRY GRAY

Ab7 Ab6 Ab+ Ab Bb9 Eb7 Ab Bb7
That old string of pearls a - la Wool - worth.
It's a string of kiss - es for ba - by.
8va bassa
loco
Eb Ebmaj7 Eb7 Eb6 Eb+ Eb Eb+ Eb6 Eb7
'Til that hap - py day in Spring when you I buy
I found a love so sub - lime, right in that
Ebmaj7 Eb Ebmaj7 Eb7 Eb6 Eb+ Eb F9 Bb7
the wed - ding ring, Please A STRING OF PEARLS a - la
old five and dime, with A STRING OF PEARLS a - la
Eb6 Bb7 Eb6 D6 Eb6
1. 2.
Wool - worth. Wool - worth.
Wool - worth. Wool - worth.
ff

A SUNDAY KIND OF LOVE

Words and Music by
BARBARA BELLE, LOUIS PRIMA,
ANITA LEONARD and STAN RHODES

F6
Am7
A♭m7
Gm7
C7♭9
Am7
D7♭9
love that's on the square._ Can't seem to find some - bod - y to care._
Gm7
B♭m6
Am7
D7
Gm7
C7+5
Gm7/C bass
I'm on a lone - ly road that leads me no - where._ I need a Sun - day kind of
F6
Cm7
F9
love._ I do my Sun - day dream - ing and
Cm7
F7♭9
B♭6
Cm7
F7♭9
B♭6
all my Sun - day schem-ing ev - 'ry min - ute, ev - 'ry hour,_ ev - 'ry day. I'm

G9 Dm7 G9 Dm7 G7♭9 C9 F♯dim
hop - ing to dis-cov - er a cer - tain kind of lov - er, who will show me the way._
Gm7 Tacet F6 Am7 A♭m7 Gm7 C7♭9 Am7 D7♭9
_ My arms need some-one to en - fold,_ to keep me warm when Mon-days are cold,_
Gm7 B♭m6 Am7 D7 Gm7 C7+5 Gm7/C bass
a love for all my life to have and to hold._ I want a Sun - day kind of
1. F6 D7♭9 Gm7 Tacet 2. F6 Gm7 B♭m6 Fmaj7
love. I want a love._
3
rit.

THIS TIME THE DREAM'S ON ME

Words by
JOHNNY MERCER

Music by
HAROLD ARLEN

Am7 D7 G G♯dim D7 add B
THIS TIME THE DREAM'S ON ME. You'll take my
G Em Am7 G♯dim Am7
hand and you'll look at me a - dor - ing - ly,
F♯dim D7 add B B7 E7 Am7 D7-9 G F F♯
But as things stand, THIS TIME THE DREAM'S ON ME.
G G+ A♯dim add D A♯dim A B7 +5 B7
It would be fun to be cer - tain that I'm the
espress.

Bm7
E7
G♯dim
Em6
Cm6
one, to know that I at least sup-
G
A7+5
A7
D7
G♯dim
D7
add B
G
Em
ply the shoulder-er you cry up-on. To see you through
Am7
G♯dim
Am7
F♯dim
D7
add B
B7
E7
till you're ev-'ry-thing you want to be, It can't be true, but
A7
+5
Am7
D7
1.
G
F
F♯
G
D7 add B
2.
G
Cm6
G
THIS TIME THE DREAM'S ON ME. Somewhere, some- ME.
rall.
a tempo

THAT LUCKY OLD SUN
(Just Rolls Around Heaven All Day)
Lyric by
HAVEN GILLESPIE
Music by
BEASLEY SMITH
Moderately
C Am Fm C F
mf
Up in the morn-in' out on the job, work like the dev-il for my
C G7 C F6 C Am Fm6
pay, But That Luck-y Old Sun has noth-in' to do but
C G7 C Am Fm
roll a-round heav-en all day. Fuss with my wom-an toil for my kids,
C F C G7 C F6
Sweat 'til I'm wrin-kled and gray, While That Luck-y Old Sun has
C Am Fm6 C Dm7 C F C
noth-in' to do but roll a-round heav-en all day. Good

Am Em F6 C Am G7 C
Lawd a - bove, can't you know I'm pin - in', Tears all in my eyes; Send
Am Em F6 C Cmaj7 Am D7
down that cloud with a sil - ver lin - in', Lift me to Par - a -
Dm7 G7 C Am Fm
dise. Show me that riv - er, Take me a - cross and
C F C G7 C F6
wash all my trou - bles a - way, Like That Luck - y Old Sun, give me
C Am Fm6 C Dm7
noth - in' to do but roll a - round heav - en all
1. C
day.
2. C F6 C
day.

THEY'RE EITHER TOO YOUNG OR TOO OLD

Words by
FRANK LOESSER

Music by
ARTHUR SCHWARTZ

Brighter tempo
C7 Gm7 C7 Gm7 C7 Gm7 C7 C Bass
f
REFRAIN
F C7 F C7
1. They're eith-er too young or too old, They're eith-er too gray or too
2. eith-er too warm or too cold, They're eith-er too fast or too
3. eith-er too bald or too bold, I'm down to the wheel-chair and
p-mf
F F♯dim Gm7 C7 F Am Bdim C9 C7
grass-y green, The pick-in's are poor and the crop is lean, What's
fast a-sleep, So, dar-ling, be-lieve me, I'm yours to keep, There
bass-i-net, My heart just re-fus-es to get up-set, I
Gm7 C7 Gm7 C7 F
good is in the arm-y, What's left will nev-er harm me. They're eith-er too old
is-n't an-y grav-y, The grav-y's in the Na-vy. They're eith-er too fresh.
sim-ply can't com-pel it to, With no ma-rines to tell it to. I'm eith-er their first

C7
F
Dm6
or too young, So dar - ling, you'll nev - er get stung.
or too stale, There is no a - vail - a - ble male.
breath of spring, Or else I'm their last lit - tle fling.
E7
A
E7
A
E
To - mor - row I'll go hik - ing with that Ea - gle Scout un - less I
I will con - fess to one ro - mance I'm sure you will al - low, He
I eith - er get a fos - sil or an ad - o - les - cent pup, I
A
E7
A
E7
A
C7
F
get a call from grand - pa for a snap - py game of chess. I'm find - ing it eas -
tries to ser - e - nade me but his voice is chang - ing now. I'm find - ing it eas -
eith - er have to hold him off or have to hold him up. The bat - tle is on,
C7
F
Dm6
B♭6
Dm
Gm7
C7
1.-2.
F
G♯dim
Gm7
C7
y to stay good as gold.
y to keep things con - trolled. They're eith - er too young or too old. They're
but the fort - ress will hold. They're

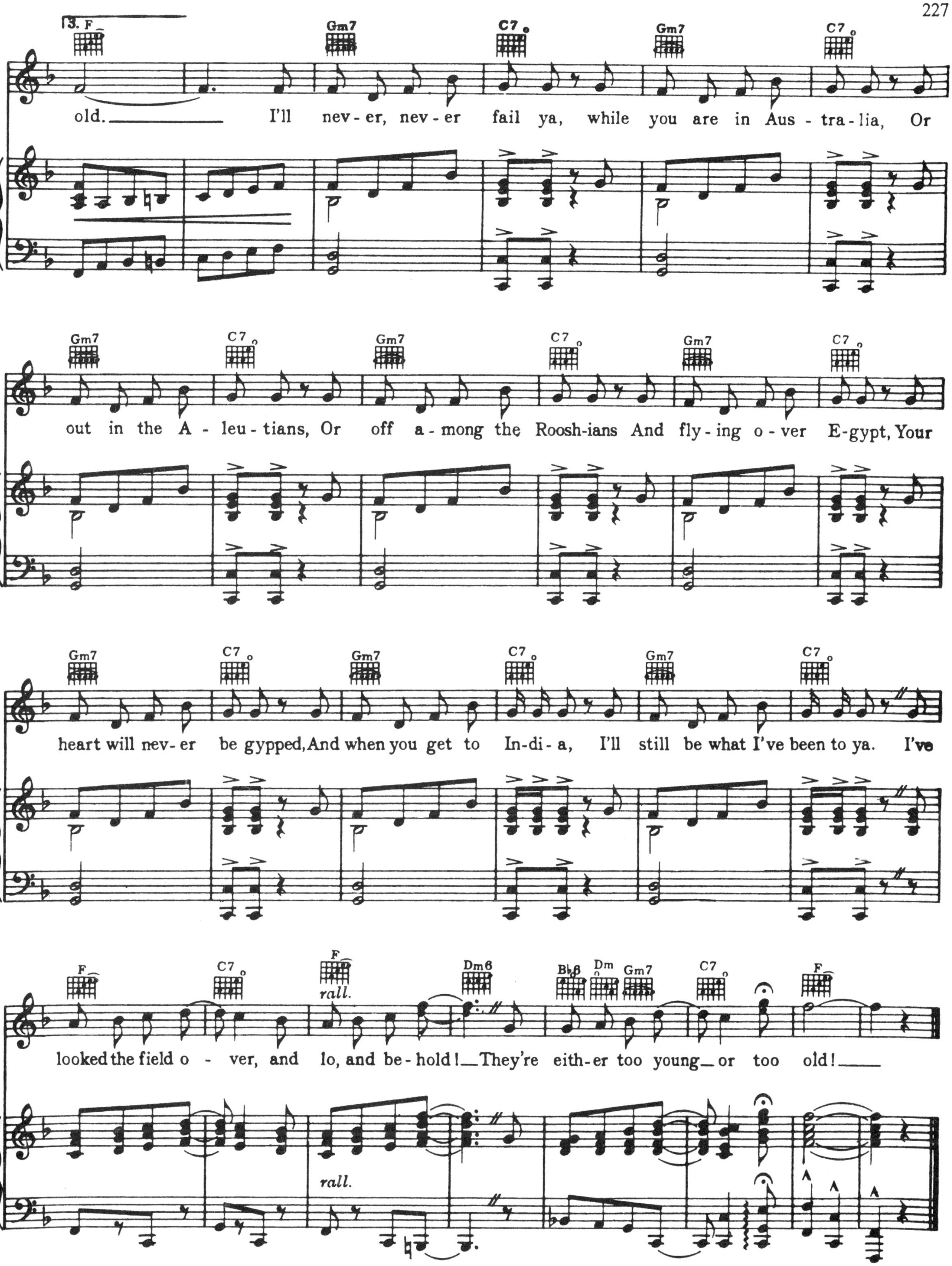

old.—— I'll nev-er, nev-er fail ya, while you are in Aus-tra-lia, Or

out in the A-leu-tians, Or off a-mong the Roosh-ians And fly-ing o-ver E-gypt, Your

heart will nev-er be gypped, And when you get to In-di-a, I'll still be what I've been to ya. I've

looked the field o-ver, and lo, and be-hold!—They're eith-er too young—or too old!——

THIS HEART OF MINE

Words by
ARTHUR FREED

Music by
HARRY WARREN

Db
Gm7
C7
F
Em7
A7
Dm
rall.
Gm
Dm7
G7
dreamed of gay a - mours; At dawn I woke up sing - ing sen - ti - men - tal ov - er-
rall.
C9
Tacet
Fmaj7
a tempo
F
E
Gm7
C7
Gm7
C9
Gdim
tures. THIS HEART OF MINE is gay - ly danc - ing now; I taste the
a tempo
Am7
F
Fmaj7
F
Am7
Cdim
Gm7
C7
Am
Gm7
Db7
F
with great breath & conviction
cresc.
wine of real ro - manc - ing now; Some-how, this cra - zy world has
cresc.
Cm
D7-9
Abm
D7
small notes ad lib.
Cdim
Gm
Bbm
F
Dm
ta - ken on a won - der - ful de - sign, As long as life en - dures its
G9
Tacet
Bbm
rall. e dim.
C7
1
F
a tempo
Tacet
mf
2
F
Tacet
F#7
B♮7
F
yours, THIS HEART OF MINE. THIS HEART OF MINE.
l.h.
rall. e dim.
a tempo
mf
dim. e rall.
ppp

TIME AFTER TIME

Words by
SAMMY CAHN

Music by
JULE STYNE

Moderato

mf

C Am Dm7 G7 C Em Dm7 G7

TIME AF-TER TIME I tell my - self that I'm so
Know what I know the pass-ing years will show you've

mp

C 1. Am Dm E7sus4 E7 D E7

luck - y to be lov - ing you, So
kept my love so

Am Am7 F♯m7-5 B7 Em Em7-5 A+ A7

luck - y to be the one you run to see in the

Dm
Dm7
G7sus4
G7
Dm7
G7
eve - ning when the day is through. I on - ly
2. C7sus4
C7
F
Fm6
C
young, so new. And TIME AF - TER
F♯m7-5
Fm6
Em7
Am
D7
D7sus4
D7
C
Am
TIME you'll hear me say that I'm so luck - y to be
Dm7
G7
C
Em
Dm7
G7
C
lov - ing you.

TILL THEN

Words and Music by
GUY WOOD, EDDIE SEILER and SOL MARCUS

Gm6
A7+5
Edim
B♭6
Bdim
F6
D7♭9
Gm
B♭m
when it will be, one day we'll be to-geth-er a-gain, please wait TILL
C9
Edim
Fmaj.7
F6
Gm7
C9
C7+5
Fmaj.7
F6
THEN. Our dreams will live tho' we are a-part, our love I know will
Gm6
A7+5
Edim
B♭6
Bdim
F6
D7♭9
keep in our hearts, TILL THEN please think of me lov-ing-ly, and
Gm
C9
F
E7
Am
E7
wait for me. Al-though there are o-ceans we must cross, and

Am
Bm7
E7
Am
E7
mountains that we must climb, I know ev-'ry gain must have a loss, so
Am7
Gm7
C9
Edim
Fmaj.7
F6
Gm7
C9
C7+5
pray that our loss is noth-ing but time. TILL THEN let's dream of what there will be, TILL
Fmaj.7
F6
Gm6
A7+5
Edim
B♭6
Bdim
Fmaj.7
Cm6
Adim
THEN we'll call on each mem-o - ry, TILL THEN when I will hold you a - gain, please
mf
1. Gm7
C9
F
D♭7
C7
2. Gm7
C7
F
wait TILL THEN. TILL wait TILL THEN.
rall.
f

THE TROLLEY SONG

Lyric by
HUGH MARTIN

Music by
RALPH BLANE

Brightly

Eb6

mf

"Clang, clang, clang," went the trol - ley,
"Chug, chug, chug," went the mo - tor,

Fm7 Bb7

"Ding, ding, ding," went the bell,
"Bump, bump, bump," went the brake,

Eb7 Ab6 Abmaj7 Abm 4 fr.

"Zing, zing, zing," went my heart - strings, For the
"Thump, thump, thump," went my heart - strings, When he

Eb6 Cm7 Fm7 Bb7 Eb6

8va loco 1.

mo - ment I saw him I fell.
smiled, I could feel the car shake.

f dim

2.
Fm7
Bb7
Eb6
mp
He tipped his hat, and took a seat He said he
Fm7
Bb7
Eb6
Am7-5
hoped he had-n't stepped up-on my feet, He asked my name,
D7
Gm7
Bbm
F
Gm7
C7
I held my breath, I could-n't speak be-cause he scared me half to
F7sus4
F7
Fm7
Bb7-9
Eb6
mf
death. "Buzz, buzz, buzz," went the buzz-er,
Fm7
Bb7
"Plop, plop, plop," went the wheels,

Eb7
Eb9
Eb7
Ab
4 fr.
Abm
4 fr.
Eb6
"Stop, stop, stop," went my heart - strings, As he start - ed to
Bb7-9
Eb
Abm6
Eb6
Gbdim
leave I took hold of his sleeve with my hand, And as
Fm7
Bb9
Edim
Fm7
Bb7
if it were planned He stayed on with me and it was
Eb6
Ab6
G7
Cm
grand, Just to stand with his hand hold - ing mine,
Fm7
Bb9
Eb6
8va
To the end of the line.
f

YOU ALWAYS HURT THE ONE YOU LOVE

Words and Music by
DORIS FISHER and
ALLAN ROBERTS

Gb9 F9 Cm Cm7
hurt at all. You al - ways take the sweet - est
F7 F+ Bb Bb
rose, And crush it till the pet - als fall. You al - ways
Bb7 Eb C7 F9
break the kind - est heart, with a hast - y word you can't re - call.
F7 Bb Bbmaj7 A7 Cm6 G7
So if I broke your heart last night, It's be -
C7 F Fmaj7 F7 1 Bb Cm7 Ebm6 F7 2 Bb
cause I love you most of all. YOU

YOU MAKE ME FEEL SO YOUNG

Words by
MACK GORDON

Music by
JOSEF MYROW

Medium Tempo (with a lilt)

B♭
B♭m
B♭dim
Gm7
C9
F7
do the cause of it all is you.
B♭
Fdim
Cm7
F7
B♭
Fdim
You make me feel so young,
You make me feel so
p-mf
Fm7
F7
B♭
B♭7
B♭7+
E♭maj7
Cm7
spring has sprung,
And ev-'ry time I see you grin, I'm such
Dm7
Gm7
C7
F7
B♭
Fdim
a hap-py in-di-vid-u-al.
The mo-ment that you speak,

Cm7
F7
B♭
Fdim
Fm7
F7
I wan-na go play hide and seek,
B♭
B♭7
B♭7
E♭maj7
Cm7
Dm7
Gm7
C7
F7
I wan-na go and bounce the moon, just like a toy bal-loon.
B♭7
B♭dim
B♭7
E♭dim
You and I are
B♭7
B♭dim
Fm7
B♭7
E♭dim
just like a coup-le of tots,
run-ning a-cross a

Gm7
Bbdim
Eb
Cm
G7
Cm
C7
F7
Cm7
F7
Cb
Bb
mead-ow, pick - ing up lots of for - get - me - nots.
Fdim
Cm7
F7
Bb
Fdim
You make me feel so young. You make me feel there are
Fm7
F7
Bb
Bb+
Ebmaj7
Ebm
songs to be sung, bells to be rung, and a won - der - ful fling to be
Bb
Dm6
Fdim
Cm7
F7
Bb
Dm6
Fdim
flung. And e - ven when I'm old and gray,

Cm7
F7
D7+
D7
G7-9
I'm gon-na feel the way I do to - day, 'cause
Cm
G7
Cm
C7
F7
B♭
Gm7
Cm7
F7
F7+
1.
You make me feel so young.
ff
B♭
Gm7
Cm7
F7
F7+
B♭
Gm7
2.
young.
Cm7
F7
F7+
B♭

YOU'LL NEVER KNOW

Words by
MACK GORDON

Music by
HARRY WARREN

Gm
Gm7
C7
F
You'll nev-er know just how much I care.
1. And if I tried, I still could-n't hide my
2. You said good-bye, no stars in the sky re-
Gm
Gm7
C7
Gm
Gm7
C7
love for you. You ought to know, for have-n't I told you
fuse to shine. Take it from me, it's no fun to be a-
F
Db7
Gm
G7
C7
F
Db7
so, a mil-lion or more times? 1. You went a-way and my heart went
lone, with moon-light and mem-'ries. 2.

Gm
Gm7
C7
with you, I speak your name in my ev - 'ry
D7
Am7
Ddim
D7
Ddim
D7
Gm
D
Bbm6
prayer. If there is some oth-er way to prove that I love you, I
F
A7
Cm
D7
Gm
G7
C7
swear I don't know how. You'll nev-er know if you don't know
1.
F
Fdim
Gm7
C7+
2.
F
Db7
F
now.
now.

YOU STEPPED OUT OF A DREAM

Lyric by
GUS KAHN

Music by
NACIO HERB BROWN

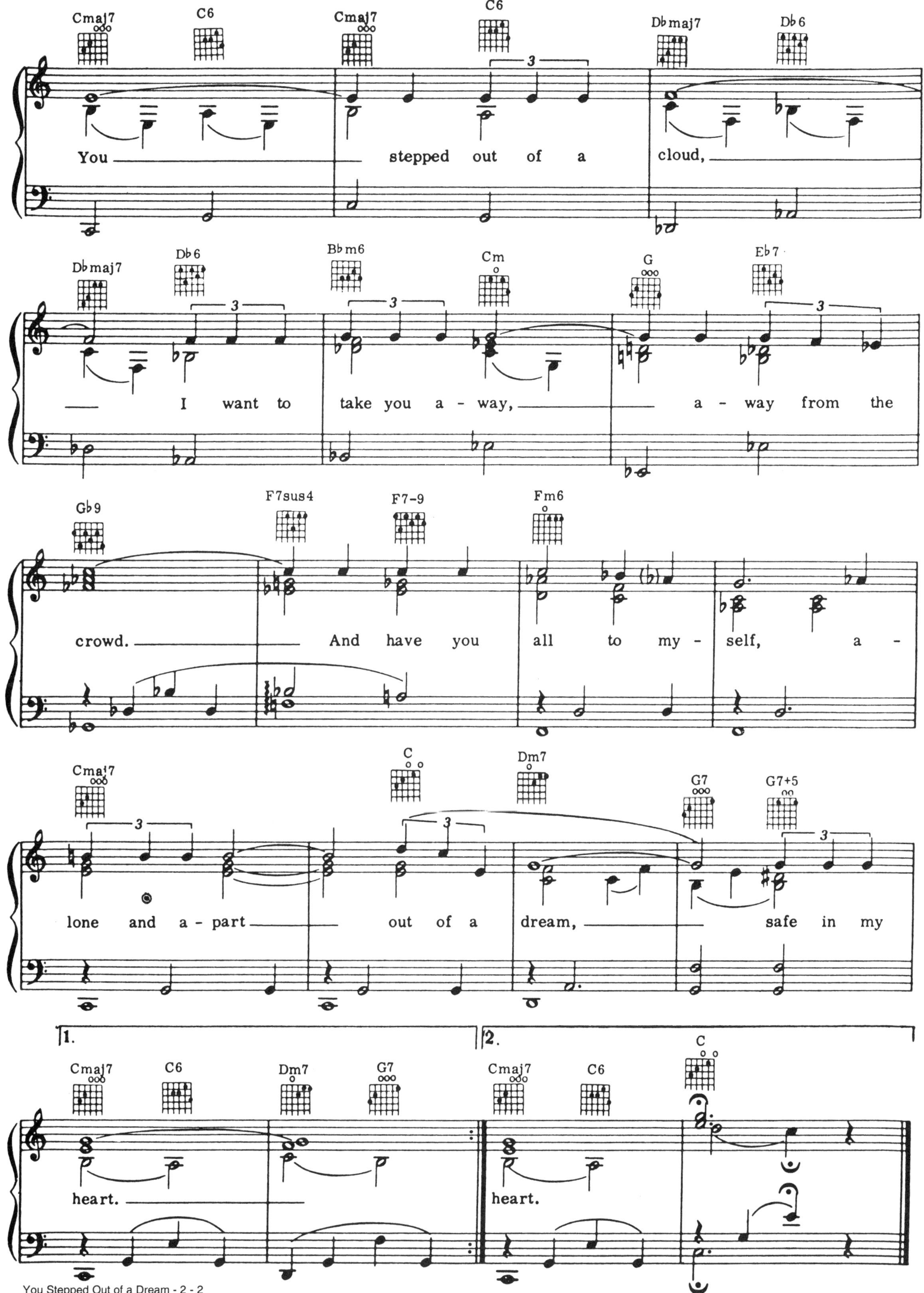
Cmaj7
C6
Cmaj7
C6
D♭maj7
D♭6
You stepped out of a cloud,
D♭maj7
D♭6
B♭m6
Cm
G
E♭7
I want to take you a - way, a - way from the
G♭9
F7sus4
F7-9
Fm6
crowd. And have you all to my - self, a -
Cmaj7
C
Dm7
G7
G7+5
lone and a - part out of a dream, safe in my
1.
2.
Cmaj7
C6
Dm7
G7
Cmaj7
C6
C
heart.
heart.

YOU'D BE SO NICE TO COME HOME TO

Words and Music by
COLE PORTER

Bb7 Eb Bb Eb7 Ab
not that you're rar - er Than as - par - a - gus out of sea - son, No, my
Bb Eb Cm6 Ebdim. Eb Fdim. D7 C
dar - ling, this is the reas - on Why you've got to be mine:
rit p mf
F E7 Am
Refrain (rather slow with feeling)
Dm6 E7 Am E7
ten. ten.
You'd be so nice to come home to,
p - mf a tempo
Am C7 F C+
You'd be so nice by the fire,

F
Am
Dm7
B7(♭5)
E7
While the breeze, on high, sang a
D dim.
Am
G7
Am6
F7
B7
lull - a - by, You'd be all that I could de -
mf
E
B7
E
D
E7
Am
Dm6
E7
sire, Un - der stars, chilled by the
p
Am
E7
Am
3
C7
win - ter, Un - der an Aug - ust moon,
cresc.

F C+ F A Dm
Burn - ing a - bove, You'd be
C dim. C F Fm6
so nice, You'd be par - a - dise to come
cresc.
mf espr.
1. C Ab7 D7 G7 C F E7
home to and love. You'd be
f
mf
2. C Ab7 D7 G7 C
home to and love.
f espr.
p

SUNDAY, MONDAY OR ALWAYS

Lyric by
JOHNNY BURKE

Music by
JIMMY VAN HEUSEN

Dm G G+ C7 F Fm6 G7
Sun-day, Mon-day or al-ways, No need to tell me now what
C E♭dim F Fm6 G7
makes the world go 'round, When at the sight of you my
C A7 C♯dim Dm7 G7 C Gm6 A7
heart be-gins to pound and pound, And what am I to do, Can't I be with you,
Dm G G+ C Cmaj7 C♯dim C Cmaj7
Sun-day, Mon-day or Al-ways? Al-ways?

D7
G7
C
B7
jeal - ous, dear, Al - read - y of Phil and Frank and Fred - dy, I
B7
E
G7
want to be your stead - y beau, So,
Dm7
G7
Cmaj7
Am
Dm
G7
G+
Won't you tell me when we will meet a-gain, Sun - day, Mon-day or
C
A9
C#dim
Dm7
G7
Cmaj7
Am
al - ways? If you're sat - is - fied, I'll be at your side,